THE INFLUENCE OF ARISTOTLE'S "POLITICS" AND "ETHICS" ON SPENSER

BY

WILLIAM FENN DeMOSS

AMS PRESS
NEW YORK

8 21
S 748 Y
D 387 ι

Reprinted from the edition of 1920, Chicago
First AMS EDITION published 1970
Manufactured in the United States of America

International Standard Book Number: 0-404-02077-1

Library of Congress Card Catalog Number: 72-123758

AMS PRESS, INC.
NEW YORK, N.Y. 10003

PREFACE

The main part of this thesis, the discussion of Aristotle's influence on the *Faerie Queene*, was written in reply to an article by Ambassador J. J. Jusserand, in *Modern Philology*, Volume III, and was published in the same journal in May and September of 1918.

I am principally indebted to my teachers, Professors John Matthews Manly and Charles Read Baskervill, who have made valuable suggestions, and to my wife, Irene C. DeMoss, who has rendered valuable assistance, and whose intelligent interest has been a source of inspiration.

CONTENTS

INTRODUCTION

The age in which Spenser lived must be kept in mind by him who would understand Spenser's works. Like other men of genius, Spenser was greatly influenced by his time.

The central purpose of the *Faerie Queene*, set forth in the famous letter to Raleigh, is a case in point. Spenser tells us, "The generall end . . . . of all the booke is to fashion a gentleman or noble person in vertuous and gentle discipline." This purpose, together with Spenser's plan for carrying it out, strongly reflects the outlook which, in the Renaissance, had been produced by the study of philosophy. The problem which Spenser undertakes was regarded, both at home and abroad, as of paramount importance.[1] All serious writers of the Renaissance had written educational treatises more or less like the *Faerie Queene*. Such are Skelton's *Magnyfycence*, Elyot's *Governour*, Wilson's *Rhetorique*, Castiglione's *Courtier* (translated into English in 1561), and Ascham's *Schoolmaster*. These works, like Spenser's, teach virtues and have in view the ideal man. The novels of the period, for example Lyly's *Euphues* and Sidney's *Arcadia*, reflect the same serious purpose. The esteem in which such studies were held is indicated by the fact that Ascham, in his *Schoolmaster*, approved heartily of Castiglione's *Courtier*, and Sidney carried the *Courtier* always in his pocket when he went abroad.[2] The teaching of morals, including manners, was of vital interest. Erasmus, that typical figure of the Renaissance, held moral and religious training to be the highest purpose of all right education. The systematic teaching of morals, from ethical writers, historians, and poets, formed an important part of a classical education in the Renaissance.[3] British schools, including Cambridge and Oxford universities, gave much attention to the teaching of morals and

---

[1] See J. J. Jusserand's *A Literary History of the English People*, II (London and New York, 1906), 476.

[2] See W. H. Woodward, *Education during the Renaissance*, Cambridge, 1906, p. 295.

[3] See Woodward, *op. cit.*, p. 125.

1

manners.[1] Again, the aristocratic element in Spenser's purpose—
the design to "fashion a gentleman or noble person"—reflects the
spirit of the Renaissance. Elyot writes to teach virtues to those
who are to have "authority in a weal public."[2] Skelton's hero is a
prince. Castiglione's courtier and statesman is of noble birth.
Lyly's *Euphues* is aristocratic, as is also Sidney's *Arcadia*. The conception that poetry should teach, implied in Spenser's purpose,
shows the influence of the Renaissance. It has its classical basis
in Aristotle (*Ethics* and *Politics*) and in Horace. Once more, the
omniscience which Spenser's purpose requires of a gentleman or
noble person reflects the Renaissance. The Renaissance, with the
"perfyte man" in view, felt that a nobleman should know well-
nigh everything.[3] This belief, drawn from the ancients, largely
from Aristotle, was encouraged by the example of the court during
the reigns of the learned Henry VIII and Elizabeth. "Never,"
says Roger Ascham, "has the English nobility been so learned."[4]
Spenser, as is shown in his letter to Raleigh, has it in mind to fashion
a gentleman, or noble person, 'perfected' in all virtues, both moral
and political—perfect in morals, manners, divinity, and statesman-
ship—the perfect man.

Another thing which shows how Spenser was influenced by his
time is his choice of a master. In telling, in the letter to Raleigh,
how he intends to "fashion a gentleman," he says, "I labour to
pourtraict in Arthure, before he was king, the image of a brave
knight, perfected in the twelve private morall vertues, as Aristotle
hath devised, the which is the purpose of these first twelve bookes:
which if I finde to be well accepted, I may be perhaps encoraged, to
frame the other part of polliticke vertues in his person, after that hee
came to be king," etc. From this it would seem that Spenser
intended to follow not only Aristotle's treatment of the moral virtues
but also his discussion of politics.

Aristotle and Plato were the great teachers of the Renaissance.
There were, to be sure, attacks upon Aristotle. But people attack
what is important. Besides, these attacks would have little influence

[1] See Jusserand, *op. cit.*, II, 49 ff.
[2] See also *Ibid.*, p. 67.
[3] *Ibid.*, pp. 65 ff.   [4] *Ibid.*, p. 73.

upon the conservative Spenser. The popularity of Aristotle in 1520 is proved by the daybook of John Dorne, bookseller, which shows several sales in that year.¹ We know that Aristotle was popular in 1551, a year or two before Spenser's birth, and in 1598, the year before Spenser's death. In 1551 a series of lectures on Aristotle was delivered at Cologne; and at this same period, as Roger Ascham tells us, Aristotle and Plato were read by English children, in Greek.² In 1598, as the *Stationers' Register* shows, there was a translation of Aristotle into English.³ Cambridge University, as Mulcaster tells us, had, in the reign of Henry VIII, taught the old axioms of Aristotle, "till in process of time good letters were brought in." The new course of study included Mathematics, etc., "as also Aristotle in a new dress, and some skill in the Greek Tongue."⁴ Another thing which shows Renaissance regard for Aristotle is the influence of the *Ethics* and *Politics* on educational treatises and other works of the time. Elyot's *Governour* draws freely upon Aristotle. Moreover, the author recommends that by the time the boy is seventeen years old he shall have read to him moral philosophy, especially Aristotle's *Ethics*, Books I and II, to teach him "reason."⁵ Skelton's *Magnyfycence* shows Aristotelian influence, as does also Jonson's *Cynthias Revels*.⁶ Sidney's *Arcadia* certainly reflects Aristotle. Wilson's *Arte of Rhetorique* is largely from Aristotle. Ascham's *Schoolmaster* is strongly Aristotelian, and Castiglione's *Courtier* is almost wholly from Aristotle. This is only a little of the evidence that could be adduced to show how the Renaissance regarded Aristotle. Woodward, in his *Education during the Renaissance*, points out that the Renaissance held "three salient characteristics" of the perfect man: (1) Aristotle's μεγαλοψυχία, Magnanimity, or Highmindedness; (2) Aristotle's μεγαλοπρέπεια, or Magnificence; and (3) Aristotle's φρόνησις, Prudence, or Reason.⁷

¹ *Ibid.*, p. 55.
² *Ibid.*, pp. 74–75.
³ *Ibid.*, p. 373.
⁴ "Babees Book," E.E.T.S., ed. Furnivall, Forewords, p. xxxix.
⁵ W. H. Woodward, *Education during the Renaissance*, Cambridge, 1906, p. 289.
⁶ See C. R. Baskervill, *English Elements in Jonson's Early Comedy*, Austin, Texas, 1911. See also R. L. Ramsay's edition of Skelton's *Magnyfycence*, E.E.T.S., pp. xxxii–xxxviii.
⁷ Pp. 261–62, Cambridge, 1906.

Again, Spenser's mingling of classic and sacred teachings, most notably in Book I, where he treats Holiness as a moral virtue,[1] is but another example of how he was influenced by his time. In the Renaissance men came to regard the great classical teachers almost as saints. Church fathers and divines made use of the teachings of Plato, and especially of Aristotle. As Jusserand puts it, "Christian and pagan ideas mingle; the notion of sacrilege fades; men of culture call the mass 'Sacra Deorum'; Pulci dedicates his second canto to the 'sovereign Jupiter crucified for us.'"[2] And we hear Erasmus say of the noble Socrates, "I can ofttimes scarcely refrain from saying, 'Saint Socrates, pray for us.'"[3]

Finally, the allegorical interpretation which Spenser puts upon Homer, Virgil, and others shows the English poet in agreement with his age. In the letter to Raleigh, Spenser says:

> I have followed all the antique Poets historicall, first Homere, who in the Persons of Agamemnon and Ulysses hath ensampled a good governour and a vertuous man, the one in his Ilias, the other in his Odysseis: then Vergil, whose like intention was to doe in the person of Aeneas, ...

Erasmus shows the Renaissance tendency to see allegory everywhere. He says, "Homeric and Virgilian poems will not be of indifferent use to thee if thou rememberest that they were entirely allegorical."[4] Erasmus sees allegory and holiness in everything—even in Horace. Elyot says that Homer, "from whom as from a fountain proceded all eloquence and lernyng," offered "instruction for politic governance of people."[5] Gavin Douglas strives to discover the mysterious meaning which he is sure is concealed in Virgil's words. He sees in Aeneas the "just perfyte man." For him each one of Aeneas' adventures holds a moral lesson; for what poets feign, he reasons, ever "bein full of secreyt onderstanding under hyd sentense or figur."[6] And Fulke Greville, the intimate friend of Sidney, is certain that under the poetical trappings of Sidney's *Arcadia* are concealed profound moral intentions. He says, "In all these creatures of his making, his intent and scope was to turn the barren philosophy

---

[1] Cf. the letter to Raleigh.
[2] *Op. cit.*, II, 15.
[3] *Ibid.*, II, 8.
[4] Jusserand, *op. cit.*, II, 8.
[5] *Ibid.*, p. 68.
[6] *Ibid.*, pp. 130 ff.

precepts into pregnant images of life."[1] This Renaissance outlook
was produced in some measure by Plato's practice of writing alle-
gories. But Plato was rather hostile to poets, considering them
incompetent to teach. This outlook comes really from Aristotle,
who justifies not only this outlook in general, but also Spenser's
interpretation of Homer in particular. Aristotle regarded the poets
as moral and political teachers. In fact he drew his conceptions in
the *Ethics* and *Politics* largely from the Greek poets, especially from
Homer. Spenser's conception that Homer is to be interpreted
allegorically, and that he represented in Agamemnon "a good
governour" and in Ulysses "a vertuous man," is justified by Aristotle
as follows: Aristotle, in teaching the great central idea of his moral
philosophy, the idea that a virtue is a mean between extremes, that
prudence, or reason, is the determiner of the mean, and that one
must keep farthest from the more dangerous of the two extremes by
veering toward the less dangerous—in teaching this, Aristotle
quotes the advice given·to Ulysses preparatory to his sailing between
Scylla and Charybdis, advice afterward repeated and followed by
Ulysses. The part quoted is the admonition to Ulysses to keep far
from Charybdis, the more dangerous of the two:

> Far from this smoke and swell keep thou thy bark.

The account of the *Odyssey* shows that Ulysses is to take reason for
his guide, and to shun Charybdis by going close to Scylla.[2] Here is a
justification not only for allegorical interpretation, but also for taking
Ulysses as a representation of the "vertuous man." The case is
no less clear for Agamemnon as "a good governour." Nor is there
any doubt that Aristotle took Homer seriously as a teacher of politics.
In the *Politics* he is discussing the Lacedemonian form of kingship,
which is held to be a model. After describing it he says, "*Such is
the evidence of Homer.* For although Agamemnon patiently endured
reproaches in the assemblies, when the army was in the field his
authority extended to life and death. Thus his [Agamemnon's]
words are. . . . ." Here he quotes Homer.[3] Again, in a passage

---

[1] *The Life of the Renowned Sir Philip Sidney*, London, 1652, p. 18.

[2] *N. Eth.*, ii, ix, and *Odyssey*, xii, especially 219–20. I refer to and quote J. E. C.
Welldon's translation of Aristotle's *Nicomachean Ethics* and *Politics*.

[3] *Politics*, Book IV, chap. xiv.

plainly implying that Agamemnon had both virtue and wisdom, Aristotle quotes the prayer which Homer puts into the mouth of Agamemnon, "Would I had ten such councillors as Nestor."[1] Yet again, in the *Ethics*, in the discussion of Friendship, where he describes the three kinds of polities and the kind of friendship appropriate to each, Aristotle illustrates his conception of the ideal king by quoting Homer. He says, "He [the good king] treats his subjects well, as being good, and as caring for their welfare, like a shepherd for the welfare of his flock, whence Homer called Agamemnon 'shepherd of the folk.'"[2] Influenced by the Renaissance tendency toward allegorical interpretation, Spenser would certainly regard such passages as significant. Spenser, whom Milton found "sage and serious," whom Milton "dared be known to think a better teacher than Scotus or Aquinas,"[3] was thinking and doing, with the added power of genius, just what his age was thinking and doing.

[1] *Politics*, III, xvii, and *Iliad*, x, 224.
[2] *N. Eth.*, VIII, xiii.
[3] *Areopagitica*.

ARISTOTLE'S INFLUENCE ON THE *FAERIE QUEENE*

In his article, entitled "Spenser's 'Twelve Private Morall Vertues as Aristotle hath Devised,'" *Modern Philology,* January, 1906, Ambassador Jusserand undertakes to prove that Spenser's solemn statement concerning the substance of the whole *Faerie Queene,* made to the poet's friend and patron Sir Walter Raleigh, at Raleigh's request, as M. Jusserand thinks, is "misleading, every word of it." Jusserand says:

> Spenser's statement [in the letter to Raleigh] that he intends "to portraict in Arthur, before he was king, the image of a brave knight, perfected in the twelve private morall vertues as Aristotle hath devised" is misleading, every word of it. There is no such definite list; Aristotle's number is not twelve, and the virtues he studies are far from being the same as those forming the basis of the *Faerie Queene.*[1]

That Jusserand's paper has not been without its influence was shown in a recent article by Professor Erskine, of Columbia University. Although Professor Erskine points out one false step in Jusserand's argument, he accepts his conclusion. In discussing "The Virtue of Friendship in the *Faerie Queene," Publications of the Modern Language Association,* XXIII (1915), 831–50, Professor Erskine asks, "Had Spenser read Montaigne, or Plutarch, or Cicero's *On Friendship,* or Aristotle's *Ethics?*" Replying to his own question he says, "He may have read them all, though M. Jusserand has taught us to suspect the Aristotle." Again, Erskine speaks of Jusserand's "having shown that Spenser did not get his list of virtues from Aristotle."

It is the purpose of the present paper to show that not only are Jusserand's arguments faulty, but his conclusion is incorrect. Jusserand makes three main arguments: first, that Spenser's and Aristotle's lists of virtues are not the same in number; second, that they are quite unlike in nature; and, third, that Spenser actually derived his virtues, and his ideas concerning a list of twelve virtues,

[1] *Modern Philology,* III, 376.

7

from Lodowick Bryskett, who in his *Discourse of Civil Life* includes a discussion of moral virtues, in which the number twelve is mentioned.

I shall reply to these three main arguments in the order in which I have stated them.

The first of Jusserand's three main arguments, that Spenser's and Aristotle's lists of virtues are not the same in number, falls into three subdivisions or arguments: first, that "Aristotle draws nowhere any dogmatic list of virtues"; second, that it is difficult to know how to count Aristotle's virtues; and, third, that "Aristotle's number is not twelve," for, count his virtues as you will, you cannot get the number twelve. I take up the last subdivision first.

Jusserand finds that nine of Aristotle's virtues are certainly virtues, but that there is some doubt concerning the remaining four: Temperance, or Self-control; Shame, or Modesty; Friendship; and Justice.[1] Jusserand says:

If we include both [Temperance and Modesty] we have a total of eleven; if we exclude both, a total of nine; if we admit Self-control alone, a total of ten. Adding arbitrarily Justice and Friendship, or only one of them . . . . we should have a total varying from ten to *thirteen;*[2] a total of twelve being perhaps the most arbitrary of all and the most difficult to reach.[3]

Now, it should be noted at the outset that a total of thirteen is exactly what we want. Spenser's total is not twelve. It is thirteen. In his letter to Raleigh, only a short distance from the assertion which Jusserand undertakes to disprove, Spenser makes the following statement:

In the person of Prince Arthure I sette forth *magnificence*[4] in particular, which vertue for that (according to Aristotle and the rest) it is the perfection of all the rest, and conteineth in it them all, therefore, in the whole course I mention the deedes of Arthure applyable to that vertue, which I write of in that booke. But of the *xii. other vertues,*[4] I make xii. other knights the patrones, for the more variety of the history.

---

[1] The fact that Spenser wrote a Book on each of these four virtues—see *Faerie Queene*, Books II, III, IV, and V—might be expected to throw some light on whether Spenser counted them as virtues or not.

Hereafter references to book, canto, and stanza of the *Faerie Queene* are given without the title of the epic.

[2] Italics mine.

[3] *Mod. Phil.*, III, 374–75.

[4] Italics mine.

So much for Jusserand's point that "Aristotle's number is not twelve." Neither is Spenser's. We may now proceed to find what is the nature of Aristotle's list of virtues, how Aristotle's virtues are to be counted, and how Spenser got his number of virtues.

In Book II, chap. vii, of the *Nicomachean Ethics*, Aristotle discusses a list of moral virtues or qualities essential to the good man. They are exactly twelve in number: (1) Courage, (2) Temperance, or Self-control, (3) Liberality, (4) Magnificence, (5) Highmindedness, (6) the mean concerning Ambition, (7) Gentleness, or Mansuetude, (8) Truthfulness, (9) Wittiness, or Jocularity, (10) Friendliness, or Courtesy, (11) Modesty, or Shame, and (12) Righteous Indignation. Concerning this discussion Aristotle says: "For the present we are giving only a rough and summary account [of the virtues], and that is sufficient for our purpose; we will hereafter determine their character more exactly."[1] We are promised, then, a careful discussion of the moral virtues "hereafter." In Book III, chaps. ix ff., Book IV, and Book V, Aristotle keeps his word. Moreover, an introductory sentence and a concluding one mark the limits of this discussion of the moral virtues as definitely as two milestones. The first two sentences of III, ix, are as follows: "Let us then resume our consideration of the several virtues and discuss their nature, the subjects with which they deal, and the way in which they deal with them. *In so doing we shall ascertain their number.*"[2] The last sentence in Book V unmistakably closes the list of moral virtues: "This then may be taken as a sufficient description of Justice, and the other moral virtues." Between these two absolutely definite limits Aristotle discusses exactly twelve good qualities or desirable means. In this careful consideration of the moral virtues, the same good qualities, or desirable means, are listed as in the less careful discussion which precedes it, with one exception: in the "rough and summary account" Righteous Indignation is included. We know from the *Rhetoric* that Aristotle decided that his discussion of this quality was false, as Envy and Malice, which he gave as its extremes, are not opposites, but compatible and coexistent.[3] In his second

---

[1] My quotations are from the translation by J. E. C. Welldon.
[2] Italics mine.
[3] See Aristotle's *Rhetoric*, Book II, chap. ix.

discussion of the moral virtues, which is to "determine their character more exactly" and "ascertain their number," he omits Righteous Indignation and adds Justice, leaving the number unchanged. Surely there is enough here to suggest the number twelve if any such suggestion were needed.

But Jusserand has difficulty in totalizing Aristotle's virtues, for he finds it hard to decide which ones are to be counted. In the first place, he contends that "Some of his virtues are only a branch or development of another virtue. . . . . Magnificence is only the same as [Liberality], but practiced by the very rich, instead of by the moderately rich, man."[1] Now it is plain that Aristotle's Magnificence and Liberality are not the same. It would be strange indeed if they were, since Aristotle treats them as two separate virtues. They are much the same in principle, as both imply being free in giving and spending. But practically they are very different. Anyone who gives to the right cause, at the right time, in the right manner, and to the right amount, considering the means of the giver, and who takes from right sources, is liberal.[2] He has to avoid the extremes of illiberality and prodigality. The magnificent man, on the other hand, must avoid the extremes of meanness and vulgar display, or bad taste. He must be a kind of artist. "The magnificent man," says Aristotle, "is like a connoisseur in art; he has the faculty of perceiving what is suitable, and of spending large sums of money with good taste. . . . . With equal expenditure he will make the result more magnificent."[3] And, as we shall see later, Magnificence includes far more than this. The poor widow who gave the mites was liberal; but the problems she had to solve in being so were very different from those of a person who is in a position to practice the virtue of Magnificence and wishes to do so.

Again, Jusserand objects, "Others . . . . are treated of quite apart, at great length; but it is not clear whether, if one wanted to do what Aristotle neglected to perform—that is, to tabulate his moral virtues—these should, or should not, be admitted in the list. Such is the case with Justice. . . . . Such is the case also with

---

[1] *Mod. Phil.*, III, 374–75.

[2] *Nicomachean Ethics*, IV, i–iii; II, vii.

[3] *Ibid.*, IV, iv–v; II, vii; *Magna Moralia*, I, 26; and *Ethica Eudemia*, III, vi.

Friendship. . . . . Aristotle has treated them apart, and shown that *he* did not include them in his regular count."[1]

Jusserand's assertion that Aristotle treated Justice apart from the other moral virtues is a misinterpretation. Justice is not separated from the preceding discussion in Books III and IV; on the contrary, it is in the closest possible way connected with it. In Book IV, chap. xiii, while discussing Truthfulness, Aristotle says: "We are not speaking of one who is truthful in legal covenants, or of all such matters as lie within the domain of justice and injustice, for these would be matters belonging to a different virtue." Again, the last sentence in Book IV is as follows: "But let us now proceed to consider Justice." Hence, one can no more draw a line between Books IV and V than between Books III and IV. Finally, the sentence which so clearly and definitely closes the discussion of the moral virtues is, as we have already seen, the last sentence in Book V: "This then may be taken as a sufficient description of *Justice*, and the *other moral virtues.*" One virtue, Friendship, Aristotle does treat "apart at great length." According to Jusserand its "admission into [Aristotle's] treatise is justified, not to say excused, on the plea that it is either a virtue or related to virtue, and that it is most necessary in life."[2] But it could hardly need a better justification.

Finally Jusserand points out: "Some, admitted into the class at one part of the work, are described elsewhere as doubtfully belonging to it. . . . . There is also a chapter on Shame (αἰδώς, Lat. *verecundia*), though 'it is not correct to call it a virtue.' But 'neither is Self-control,' adds Aristotle in the same chapter."[3] Thus Jusserand makes much of showing that Aristotle is sometimes uncertain whether a given one of his desirable means is a virtue or not— that is, whether or not it comes under a technical definition of virtue. And then, strangely enough, he expects Spenser to be severely technical when his master has not been. But Aristotle tells us plainly in Book I, chap. i, of his *Nicomachean Ethics*, and again in Book II, chap. ii, that in a discussion on ethics scientific exactitude is impossible. He answers Jusserand's objections some centuries

[1] *Mod. Phil.*, III, 374–75.
[2] *Ibid.*, p. 374.
[3] *Ibid.*, pp. 374–75.

before they were made. He says: "An educated person will expect accuracy in each subject only so far as the nature of the subject allows."[1] Jusserand overlooks the important fact that both Aristotle and Spenser are eminently practical in their aims. In Book II, chap. ii, Aristotle says: "Our present study is not, like other studies, purely speculative in its intention; for the object of our inquiry is not to know the nature of virtue but to become ourselves virtuous, as that is the sole benefit which it conveys." Spenser's statement to Raleigh of the object he had in writing the *Faerie Queene* shows the practical nature of that work: "The general end therefore of all the book is to fashion a gentleman or noble person in vertuous and gentle discipline."[2] With such a purpose, is it likely that Spenser would stop to quibble over whether such a quality as Temperance, for example, does or does not come under a technical definition of virtue? What would his gentleman be without it? Is it not reasonable that, in attempting to follow Aristotle, Spenser would take all of Aristotle's desirable means or good qualities? Whether certain of them come under a technical definition of virtue or not, they are virtues in any practical sense. And Aristotle himself regarded them as such, as is shown by the fact that he discussed them as virtues. Besides, they are absolutely necessary to a system which is to "fashion a gentleman or noble person" not only in "vertuous," but also in "gentle," discipline.

This brings us to a very simple explanation of how Spenser got his number of virtues. He simply took all of Aristotle's desirable means, or qualities essential to the good man. Now Aristotle discussed, all told, thirteen good qualities, or desirable means, as Jusserand himself observes. One of these, as Jusserand also observes, is Magnificence. Magnificence, as we saw, Spenser gives to Arthur, leaving exactly twelve others. Clearly, if one of Aristotle's virtues contains all the others, his virtues might properly be divided into "the twelve" and the *one* which includes the *twelve*.

So much for the number of Spenser's and Aristotle's virtues. We come now to Jusserand's argument that "the nature of the virtues considered by Spenser matches the Aristotelian selection

---

[1] *N. Eth.*, I, 1.

[2] Spenser's Letter to Sir Walter Raleigh, included in all editions of the *Faerie Queene*.

scarcely better than their number"[1]—a proposition which to Jusserand means that the two do not match at all.

Before discussing the nature of Spenser's virtues, it will be necessary to clear the ground somewhat by saying a word about how the *Faerie Queene* is to be interpreted. There is a notion that Spenser's episodes are unimportant. For example, Jusserand disposes of the lesson of one of Spenser's great cantos by saying, "It is only incidentally dwelt upon, forming the episode of Guyon's visit to Medina, Bk. II, c. 2."[2] And in this attitude toward the episodes Jusserand is by no means alone. Any notion that whatever is not a part of Spenser's main plot can have little to do with his meaning is based upon a misconception of the fundamental structure of Spenser's great poem. An episode filling one of Spenser's cantos—a great poem in itself—such as the one in which Guyon is taken by his Palmer (Reason or Prudence) to the house of Medina (the Mean), where the Knight of Temperance learns the fundamental conception of true Temperance, cannot be considered unimportant. Such an episode may be "only incidental" to some of the points named in Spenser's letter to Raleigh, in which the author undertakes to state the "general intention" and to give something of the plot and plan of more than half a million words, and to propose and name the contents of a second poem, which would probably[3] have contained another half million words, all in a four-page letter—a summary which disposes of the whole of the Book on Temperance in six lines. But in Spenser's development of any given virtue, such an episode is of very great importance.

It is mainly by means of the episodes that Spenser's discussion of the virtues is carried on. This fact will become clear as we proceed. We may note here, however, Spenser's direct testimony that his episodes are organic. In the Book on Courtesy, at the end of a three-canto episode showing Calidore's Courtesy among the lowly, Spenser makes it unmistakably clear that each episode in the *Faerie*

---

[1] *Mod. Phil.*, III, 375.

[2] *Ibid.*, p. 381, and note.

[3] It will be observed that Spenser does not say how many Books will be in the second part; he speaks only of "these first twelve bookes" and of "the other part." Nor does he give the number of the political virtues. Aristotle gives nowhere a list of the political virtues.

Queene represents some phase of the virtue under discussion; that the author "never is astray."[1] Again, in the Book on Justice, in introducing the account of the spousal of Florimel, Spenser assures us that he is admitting to the poem nothing save what "with this present treatise doth agree, True vertue to advance."[2] And the episode turns out to be a study in just distribution of honors, which according to Aristotle is the essence of Justice.[3]

Moreover, Spenser does not intend that his readers shall misunderstand him. "By certaine signes here set in sundry place,"[4] he aims to see to it that the *reader* "never is astray." And among the most helpful of these "signes" are the very illuminating comments of the author, oftenest at the beginning, but sometimes in the middle of a canto.[5] No one will need to be reminded of the importance of Spenser's arguments to the cantos and his proems to the books. Sometimes a few lines spoken by one of the characters throw great light on the allegory of the poem.[6] Professor Greene has truly remarked, "Only a man of abundant leisure can read the [*Faerie Queene*] as Spenser would have it read."[7] To get the meaning, one must watch not only the enveloping plot and the episodes, but also every comment, every speech, every line, every word, and, frequently, in the case of proper names, every syllable. He must read the poem intensively—minutely:

> ne let him then admire,
> But yield his sence to be too blunt and bace,
> That no'te without an hound fine footing trace.[4]

So much for the manner in which Spenser is to be interpreted. Let us now examine, in the case of each of the six virtues developed by Spenser, Jusserand's argument that Spenser's and Aristotle's virtues are unlike in nature.

---

[1] VI, xii, 1–2. Cf. I, vii, 50; II, xii, 1; III, vi, 52; VI, iii, 25; VI, ix, 1.

[2] V, iii, 3.

[3] With this canto of Spenser's Book on Justice, cf. *N. Eth.*, V, ii, and V, iv, and *Politics*, II, vii. With Braggadocchio cf. Achilles' Coward, *Politics*, II, vii.

[4] Book II, Proem, stanza 4.

[5] See I, viii, 1, or I, x, 1. Other examples will be pointed out later.

[6] See, for example, I, viii, 49.

[7] H. L. Greene, "Allegory in Spenser, Bunyan, and Swift," *Pub. Mod. Lang. Assoc.*, IV (1889), 181.

Concerning the subject of Spenser's first Book, Jusserand says: "Holiness is certainly not borrowed from Aristotle's series of moral virtues."[1] This is mere assertion, not argument. Possibly an argument is thought to lie in a supposed inconsistency between "holiness" and "moral virtues"; but if so, it should be remembered that Spenser certainly classed holiness as a moral virtue, as is shown not only by the letter to Raleigh but also by the "XII. Morall vertues" of the title-page of the *Faerie Queene*.

Again, Jusserand says that Spenser's reference to the twelve moral virtues of Aristotle was "a mere afterthought, probably, imagined after part of the poem had been written; for Spenser begins with the virtue of Holiness, conspicuously absent as we saw from Aristotle's enumeration," etc.[2] Surely it is incredible that Spenser should contemplate a great epic for years (see Spenser's letter to Harvey under date of 1580) and finally write the forty-five thousand words of the Book on Holiness without even a general notion of the plot and purpose of his poem. Besides, the fact that the machinery of the court of Gloriana and of the quests is introduced at the very beginning of Book I[3] indicates that the plan of the letter to Raleigh was not an "afterthought." But even if we were to admit that the reference to Aristotle was an afterthought, conceived after the first Book was written, it would have to fit, at least approximately. And Book I, Holiness, was one of the three which accompanied the letter to Raleigh. How could Spenser say that each of the twelve Books of the *Faerie Queene* would contain one of Aristotle's twelve moral virtues, "of which these three bookes contayn three,"[4] when the first of the three had nothing whatever to do with Aristotle? Could he expect to deceive Raleigh, Sidney, Elizabeth, and the rest of the brilliant circle for whom he wrote?

Obviously Jusserand misunderstands, or has forgotten, the meaning of Aristotle's virtue of Highmindedness, or Magnanimity; for he sees in it only "a kind of ornament applicable to all the virtues."[5] It is well known that this virtue represents Aristotle's conception of

[1] *Mod. Phil.*, III, 376.
[2] *Ibid.*, p. 381.
[3] I, i. See also canto vii, stanza 46.
[4] Letter to Raleigh.
[5] *Mod. Phil.*, III, 382.

absolute moral perfection. "The highminded man," says Aristotle, "seems to be one who thinks himself worthy of great things, and who is worthy of them. For he who thinks himself worthy of great things without being so is foolish, and no virtuous person is foolish or absurd." "There will be one particular object of his interest . . . . honor." "Highmindedness, then, has to do with honor on a great scale." "The highminded man, as being worthy of the highest things, will be in the highest degree good." "It seems that the highminded man possesses such greatness as belongs to every virtue." "It seems that Highmindedness is, as it were, the crown of the virtues, as it enhances them and cannot exist apart from them." Finally, the following sentence shows Aristotle's exalted conception of Highmindedness: "He [the highminded man] will be only moderately pleased at great honors conferred upon him by virtuous people, as feeling that he obtains what is naturally his due or even less than his due; for it would be impossible to devise an honor that should be proportionate to perfect virtue."[1]

But is the Knight of Holiness Aristotle's highminded man? Some change in the conception of the Red Cross Knight was, of course, necessary on account of the fact that he was a Christian hero. So far as possible, however, Spenser has made him conform to Aristotle's conception of Highmindedness. First, he is characterized by a high opinion of himself. For proof of his amazing self-confidence we have not only Spenser's letter to Raleigh, but also the *Faerie Queene* itself. "A tall clownishe younge man" who has never worn armor,[2] he enters the court of great Gloriana,

> Where noblest knights were to be found on earth,[3]

and to the great wonder of the Queen and the disappointment and mortification of Una, whom he proposes to help, demands the greatest of all quests, the establishment of Truth—true Christianity—and the defeat of Error and the Devil, a quest so difficult that, although great knights from all over the world have tried it, none has been able to fulfil it.[4] Assuredly he thinks himself worthy of great things. But he not only *thinks* himself worthy; he *is* worthy—as is abundantly proved, not alone by his ability to wear the Christian armor, which

---

[1] For Aristotle's discussion of Highmindedness see *Nicomachean Ethics*, IV, vii ff.
[2] Letter to Raleigh, and *F.Q.*, I, i, 1.   [3] I, iii, 28.   [4] I, vii, 45.

is the test,[1] nor by Una's later testimony concerning his great work,[2] but also by his final triumph over all enemies including the Dragon of Evil.[3] In the second place, his chief thought is the winning of great earthly honor. His "noble heart" is "with child of glorious great intent" and

> Can never rest, untill it forth have brought
> Th' eternall brood of glorie excellent.[4]

"All for prayse and honour he did fight."[5] From first to last the Knight of Holiness is in pursuit of honor. He has come to Faerie Court in the first place to seek for fame:

> prickt with courage, and thy forces pryde,
> To Faery court thou cam'st to seeke for fame.[6]

Upon our first introduction to him, at the beginning of the *Faerie Queene*, we are told:

> Upon a great adventure he was bond,
> That greatest Gloriana to him gave,
> That greatest Glorious Queene of Faerie lond,
> To winne him worship, and her grace to have,
> *Which of all earthly things he most did crave.*[7]

And when he appears in the third Book, after he has attained perfect Holiness, his character in this respect is unchanged:

> Then he forth on his journey did proceede,
> To seeke adventures, which mote him befall,
> And win him worship through his warlike deed,
> *Which alwayes of his paines he made the chiefest meed.*[8]

Nor does the Red Cross Knight seek merely great honor; he seeks the greatest of all earthly honor. Una tells him that his fight with the Dragon of Evil

> shall ye evermore renowmed make,
> *Above all knights on earth, that batteill undertake.*[9]

---

[1] Letter to Raleigh.
[2] I, vii, 47–49.
[3] I, xi.
[4] I, v, 1.
[5] I, v, 7.
[6] I, x, 66.
[7] I, i, 3. Italics in quotations from Spenser are all mine. I quote from Smith and De Selincourt's *Poetical Works of Spenser*, Oxford, 1912, but I have disregarded the italicization of proper names and followed modern usage in regard to u, v, and j.
[8] III, iv, 4.
[9] I, xi, 2.

And Heavenly Comtemplation has already told him what this great
honor is to be.   The knight is to be Saint George, famous throughout
Europe as a military saint, and the patron saint of England:

> For thou emongst those Saints, whom thou doest see,
> Shalt be a Saint, and thine owne nations frend
> And Patrone: thou Saint George shalt called bee,
> Saint George of mery England, the signe of victoree.[1]

Finally, that the Red Cross Knight's Highmindedness may be complete and convincing in Spenser's and Aristotle's[2] view, Heavenly
Contemplation explains that the knight is of high birth—

> thou springst from ancient race
> Of Saxon kings.[3]

And we know that it is by deliberate plan, not by accident, that
Spenser makes the Red Cross Knight's one great passion love of
honor.   Even Heavenly Contemplation sanctions the knight's pursuit of earthly fame.[4]   And the poet, in his own person—

> That I this man of God his godly armes may blaze[5]—

prays aid of

> The Nourse of time, and everlasting fame
> That warlike hands ennoblest with immortall name.[6]

The moral perfection which the knight attains is, no doubt, to be
expected: .

> from the first unto the last degree,
> His mortall life he learned had to frame
> In holy righteousnesse, without rebuke or blame.[7]

It is not to be overlooked that all of Spenser's great knights are
characterized by Highmindedness, as they are by all of the other
moral virtues.   This is in accordance with Aristotle's tendency to
make any given virtue include all the others, and his teaching that
"Neither greatness nor highmindedness is possible without complete
virtue."[8]   But although, on account of this close relation between
the virtues, such great knights as Guyon and Artegall are characterized by Highmindedness, none of Spenser's knights, except possibly

---

[1] I, x, 61.
[2] This statement is warranted not only by Aristotle's and Spenser's strong feeling
of aristocracy, but also by Aristotle's discussion of Highmindedness in *N. Eth.*, IV, viii.
[3] I, x, 65.   [6] I, xi, 5.
[4] I, x, 59, 60, and 62.   [7] I, x, 45.
[5] I, xi, 7.   [8] *N. Eth.*, IV, viii.

the all-perfect Arthur, can compare in Highmindedness with the Knight of Holiness. That especial emphasis should be laid on Arthur's Highmindedness would naturally result not only from the close relation between the virtues, but also from Arthur's moral perfection. But it is in Book I, where Arthur tells his dream of glory, that we are most impressed with his Highmindedness. And according to Spenser's plan in the letter to Raleigh, Arthur must, in the Book on Holiness, represent the same virtue as the Knight of Holiness: "In¹ the whole course I mention the deedes of Arthure applyable to that vertue, which I write of in that booke." Consequently, if Arthur represents Highmindedness in Book I, so must the Knight of the Red Cross. Thus it is clear that the Knight of Holiness exemplifies Aristotle's virtue of Highmindedness. Nor was Spenser doing anything unusual in thus combining pagan and sacred writings. He was only doing what many divines did both before and after him. Moreover, he was only doing what he himself did again and again in the *Faerie Queene*, sometimes in a rather surprising fashion. For example, in II, xii, 52, he compares Acrasia's Bower, falsely named the "Bowre of blis," not only to "Parnasse" and Mount Ida, but also to the Garden of Eden, the comparison being unfavorable even to Eden. Again, the marriage rites of Una and the Knight of Holiness, described in I, xii, are pagan, not Christian.¹ There is nothing surprising, however, in his combining Aristotle's Highmindedness with Christianity; for the combination is simply moral perfection (represented by the Knight of Holiness) married to Christian truth (Una).

I have discussed the case of Holiness at considerable length because it is the only one which is in any way doubtful. In Books II–VI it is certain that Spenser is consciously and deliberately following Aristotle.

The subject of Spenser's second Book is Temperance. Jusserand has to admit that "[Spenser's virtue of] Temperance truly and plainly corresponds to one of Aristotle's [virtues]."² Aristotle outlines Temperance briefly in the *Nicomachean Ethics*, II, vii, discusses it at some length in III, xiii–xv, and continues the discussion throughout

¹ See I, xii, 37.
² *Mod. Phil.*, III, 376.

most of Book VII.   Spenser, in his Book on Temperance, draws upon all three discussions.

Concerning the virtue of Spenser's third Book, Jusserand says: "Chastity may be held to have been'[one of Aristotle's virtues], if we give the word the sense of 'shame' (*verecundia*), and neglect the fact that Aristotle, while studying it, declares that this 'shame' is not a virtue."[1]   That both Spenser and Aristotle were interested in practical morality, not in whether such qualities as Temperance and Chastity are technically virtues, we have already seen.   Although Aristotle tends to make this virtue of Shame, or Modesty, all-inclusive, just as he tends to make all the others, his discussion of it in the *Nicomachean Ethics*[2] and in the *Rhetoric*[3] leaves unquestionable the fact that he means it particularly to apply to sex morality.   It is hardly necessary to state that in his Book on Chastity Spenser is discussing sex morality from the standpoint of Shame, or Modesty, on the one hand, and Shamelessness, on the other.[4]   It should be added that sex morality is also an important part of Aristotle's discussion of Temperance, including Licentiousness and Incontinence.   Aristotelian Temperance, in the strict or particular sense, applies to "meats" and "drinks" and "what are called the pleasures of love."[5] Aristotelian Shame, or Modesty, in the strict sense, applies, of course, to the last of these.   Spenser, in his Book on Chastity, drew not only upon Aristotle's discussion of Shame, or Modesty, but also upon that part of his discussion of Temperance and Incontinence which deals with sex morality.

Concerning the subjects of Spenser's fourth and fifth Books, Jusserand says: "The reader knows what the case is with Friendship and Justice."[6]   I believe he does.

Finally, concerning Courtesy, the subject of Spenser's sixth Book, Jusserand says: "Courtesy may be held to correspond, if to anything, to Aristotle's friendliness, but not without a considerable

---

[1] *Mod. Phil.*, III, 376.

[2] *N. Eth.*, II, vii; IV, xv.

[3] *Rhetoric*, II, vi, xii, and xiii.

[4] See, for example, III, i, 48.   See also, III, i, 50; III, ii, 40–41; III, iv, 45; III, v, 55; III, vii, 49; III, viii, 32; and III, xii, 24.

[5] *N. Eth.*, III, xiii.

[6] *Mod. Phil.*, III, 376.

extension and modernization of the word. . . . . Aristotle's description of friendliness best suits, however, without matching it exactly, the modern notion of courtesy."[1] The *New English Dictionary* reveals nothing inconsistent in Spenser's discussing under the name of Courtesy the virtue which Aristotle says is most *like* Friendliness. But what really counts, a comparison of Spenser's Book on Courtesy with this Near-Friendliness, shows that the two really do match. The sphere of Aristotle's Near-Friendliness is "human society, with its common life and association in words and deeds." The virtue is a mean between flattery, obsequiousness, complaisance, on the one hand, and surliness, disagreeableness, contentiousness, on the other. Aristotle says: "It most resembles Friendliness; for the person in whom it exists answers to our idea of a virtuous friend, except that friendliness includes affection as well. . . . . He will so act alike to strangers and acquaintances," etc.[2] Thus Aristotle's Near-Friendliness is a kind of Golden Rule: In your association with others, including strangers, speak to them and act toward them as a virtuous friend would do.

Spenser's virtue of Courtesy matches this Aristotelian ideal exactly. It allows neither flattery, on the one hand, nor contentiousness, on the other.[3] It consists in acting toward others as a virtuous friend would act. It should be remembered, however, that with both Aristotle and Spenser friendship includes love; and also that, in accordance with Aristotle's and Spenser's tendency to make any given virtue include all the others, Courtesy and Discourtesy will include other virtues and vices.

> For seldome yet did living creature see,
> That curtesie and manhood ever disagree.[4]

That the virtue of Spenser's sixth Book does consist in acting toward others as a true friend would act is shown by the characters and the episodes. Calidore, Tristram, Calepine, Prince Arthur, and others represent Courtesy, or Friendliness. Maleffort, Crudor, and Briana, who maltreat strangers (c. i.); the "proud discourteous knight" whom Tristram slays (c. ii); the contemptible Sir Turpine, who will not

---

[1] *Ibid.*
[2] *N. Eth.*, IV, xii.
[3] See, for example, Spenser's exposition of Calidore's Courtesy in VI, i, 2–3.
[4] VI, iii, 40.

give lodging to Calepine and his wounded lady, or help the wounded woman over the ford, and who even attacks the defenseless knight (c. iii, vi, viii); Mirabella, who delights in the sufferings of her lovers (c. vii); the "salvage nation," which preys upon strangers (c. viii, stanzas 35 ff.); and the "theeves" who lead Pastorell into captivity (c. ix, xi)—these are some of the examples of Unfriendliness, of not acting toward others as a virtuous friend would act.   And, finally, the Blatant Beast is not Slander, as it is sometimes named, nor yet the Puritans, as it is oftenest named.   It is the Spirit of Unfriendliness;[1] it is Malice, Malevolence, Envy, Despite, Slander, Contentiousness, and is represented in one place,[2] no doubt, by the most contentious element among the Puritans.   The Blatant Beast, like Duessa,

> could d'on so manie shapes in sight,
> As ever could cameleon colours new.[3]

Besides, Spenser more than once shows by the speeches of his characters, combined with the plot, that he is keeping before him Aristotle's ideal of acting toward others as a true friend would act.   For example, in VI, iii, 15, Aldine is talking to Sir Calidore, the Knight of Courtesy.   The two are strangers, having seen each other but once before.   We are told:

> In th'end his [Calidore's] kyndly *courtesie* to prove,
> He [Aldine] him by all the bands of love besought,
> And *as it mote a faithfull friend behove,*
> To safeconduct his love, and not for ought
> To leave, till to her fathers house he had her brought.

After attempting to show that the virtues of Spenser's six[4] Books are not the ones discussed by Aristotle, Jusserand contends that

---

[1] With V, xii, 28–43, and VI, i, 7–10, in which passages the Blatant Beast is identified with Envy and Detraction, the latter including Malevolence, and with VI, v, 12–22, in which the Blatant Beast is identified with Malice, Deceit, and Detraction, compare the author's comment, or literal exposition of Discourtesy, in VI, vii, 1–2.

[2] See VI, xii, 22–41; but note in VI, xii, 22 and 23, that the Blatant Beast has gone "through every place" and "through all estates," all ranks of life, before he comes to the "Clergy."

[3] IV, i, 18.

[4] M. Jusserand holds that the fragment called Book VII is not a part of the *F.Q.* Therefore, he does not discuss it.   My discussion of it will be found in the next section of this thesis.

Spenser's and Aristotle's virtues are unlike in that Aristotle treats all his virtues as means between extremes, even straining absurdly to do so, whereas Spenser treats only one of his, Temperance, as a mean, and it "only incidentally."[1] He admits that, "Either through direct or indirect borrowings, [Spenser] took from [Aristotle] his notion of the middle or virtuous state, standing between two faulty extremes." But he adds, "He did not try, as Aristotle did, to apply this theory to every virtue. It is only incidentally dwelt upon, forming the episode of Guyon's visit to Medina, Book II, c. 2."[2] This point is important; for Jusserand's criticism means that Spenser ignored, almost completely, Aristotle's fundamental conception of what a virtue is—ignored what is the most important and characteristic thing about Aristotle's moral philosophy. Let us see if he did.

Expressed in terms of method, Aristotle's moral philosophy is essentially this: (1) He develops a virtue by showing its opposites, and by discussing various phases of the virtue and of its opposites.[3] He treats a virtue as a mean between two extremes;[4] but he discusses various phases of the mean and of its extremes, and he tends to make any given virtue include all the others;[5] so that his virtues become a kind of center surrounded by many opposites.[6] (2) He gives great emphasis to what he calls "the opposite" of a virtue, and says less, and in some cases almost nothing, about the other extreme, for his mean is not arithmetical; one who aims at the mean, he says, must, like Ulysses, keep farthest from Charybdis, the more dangerous of the two extremes.[7] And (3) he makes Reason the determiner of the right course in the case of each of the moral virtues.[8]

Such is the essence of Aristotle's moral philosophy. If, as Jusserand contends, Spenser ignores one of these principles, he is certainly not following Aristotle. If, as I shall undertake to prove, he applies

[1] *Mod. Phil.*, III, 374, 381, and note.

[2] *Ibid.*, 381, and note.

[3] See *N. Eth.*, III, ix ff.; IV; and V. See also II, vii.

[4] See his definition of virtue "regarded in its essence or theoretical conception," *N. Eth.*, II, vi. See also II, viii.

[5] See his explanation of his definition of virtue, *N. Eth.*, VI, especially chaps. i and xiii.

[6] See *N. Eth.*, II, v, and II, ix.

[7] See *N. Eth.*, II, ix.   [8] *Ibid.*, II, vi.

all of these principles in his treatment of the virtues, he certainly does follow Aristotle, at least in essentials.

Spenser certainly develops the virtue of Holiness by showing its opposites, and by presenting various phases of the virtue and of its opposites. He represents Holiness by the Knight of Holiness (High-mindedness, moral perfection), Una (Christian Truth), Faith, Hope, and Charity, Heavenly Contemplation, and so on; and around these he groups Paganism, or Infidelity, "Blind Devotion"[1] (Corceca), Mo-nastic Superstition (Abessa), "Hypocrise"[2] (Archimago), Falsehood (Duessa, "faire Falsehood"[3]), False Pride or Conceit (Orgoglio and Lucifera), the Seven Deadly Sins and all the other vices, Error (the Dragon of Error in the first canto), and Satan (in Lucifera's train, and the Dragon of Evil in canto xi).

Moreover, he represents the virtue as a mean between extremes and emphasizes one extreme. Paganism, represented by the Paynim brethren Sansfoy (Unbelief), Sansjoy (Joylessness), and Sansloy (Lawlessness), is certainly one extreme in regard to Holiness. The opposite extreme is represented by Corceca ("Blind Devotion"), Abessa (Monastic Superstition), and the Satyrs who worship even Una's ass. Corceca is an ignorant, blind old woman who says thirty-six hundred prayers every day. She dares not stop mumbling her prayers. Abessa is her daughter. Again, the Knight of Holi-ness is a mean between sinful "joyaunce" and joyless faith and abstinence, though it costs him hard fighting to keep to this mean. After he has slain the Paynim Sansfoy (canto ii), he successfully resists (canto iv) the temptation to join with Duessa in the "joy-aunce" of the gay party composed of the Seven Deadly Sins. But immediately after he has resisted the joyance of sin, he is attacked by the Paynim Sansjoy, who proposes to cancel his victory over Sansfoy by taking away the shield which is the emblem of his victory.[4] He is least fortified on the side of Joylessness; we are told upon our first introduction to him that "of his cheere [he] did seeme too solemne sad."[5] Accordingly, the battle which ensues with Sansjoy is one of

---

[1] I, iii, Arg.   [2] I, i, Arg.   [3] I, ii, Arg.

[4] For the joyfulness of Faith see Spenser's description of Faith (Fidelia) in canto x, especially stanzas 12–14.

[5] I, i, 2.

the hardest of his career.[1] Once more the Knight of Holiness is, as we have already seen, Aristotle's mean of Highmindedness. He thinks himself worthy of great things and is worthy of them; he neither overestimates nor underestimates his own worth—he is neither conceited nor meanminded. Arthur also represents this mean of Highmindedness. He thinks himself worthy of great honor, and is worthy of it. He aspires to the hand of great Gloriana (Glory), but we know, not only from his moral perfection, but also from the direct testimony of Una and the Knight of Holiness, that he is worthy of her.[2] According to Aristotle, the worst case of Meanmindedness, one of the two extremes in regard to Highmindedness is the man of great worth who underestimates his own deserts—cares too little for honor. Sir Satyrane, in a measure, illustrates this extreme. We feel that he is capable of as great things as Guyon or Calidore. Yet he disappoints us; he does nothing supremely great. Although he is possessed of great worth and wins fame—"through all Faery lond his famous worth was blown"[3]—he cares nothing for great honor. He is not among those who seek quests from great Gloriana,

That glorie does to them for guerdon graunt.[4]

To represent Conceit, the other main extreme in regard to Highmindedness, two characters are drawn, one masculine and one feminine. Orgoglio (Ital. *orgoglio*, pride; cf. Gk. ὀργάω), though born of dirt and wind, and fostered by Ignaro (Ignorance), thinks himself very great. But when he is slain by the Knight of Holiness, his huge trunk collapses like a punctured bladder, showing that he is puffed up with conceit. Lucifera (the sinful mistress of the "house of Pryde"[5]) is excessively proud and supercilious, though she is only the daughter of "Griesly Pluto" and the "Queene of Hell" and is thoroughly unworthy of honor. She includes all the Seven Deadly Sins, as Highmindedness includes all the virtues. Duessa also serves to represent Conceit,[6] though her main business is to represent Falsehood; she is very proud of her beauty and finery, but when stripped

---

[1] For the importance which Spenser attaches to this battle against joylessness, see the author's comments in canto v, stanza 1.

[2] I, ix, 16, 17.   [3] I, vi, 29.   [4] I, x, 59.   [5] I, iv, Arg.

[6] Note in I, iv, 37, that Duessa rides next to Lucifera.

of false show, she proves to be only a filthy old hag.   Clearly Spenser's emphasis is on the extreme of Conceit or False Pride.

Finally, Spenser certainly makes Reason the determiner of the mean for the virtue of Holiness.   In canto ii the arch-deceiver Archimago makes the Knight of Holiness believe that his lady, Una, has stained her honor.   Enraged, the Knight deserts Una, for whom he has undertaken to slay the Dragon of Evil, and rides off alone. He has ceased to be governed by Reason.   We are told:

> The eye of [his] reason was with rage yblent.[1]

Later we see again that he is guided not by Reason, but by 'will':

> Will was his guide, and griefe led him astray.[2]

This is the beginning of all his troubles.   He now misses the mean of Highmindedness.   After a narrow escape from the House of Pride with its vices and pitiable victims, he is captured by Orgoglio (False Pride, Conceit) and languishes in his prison until rescued by Arthur (Highmindedness).   Again, in canto vii, Arthur meets the deserted Una.   In persuading her to unfold her grief, he advises her that "flesh may empaire . . . . but reason can repaire."[3]   And "his goodly reason"[4] wins.   Thus we see that both Una and the Knight of Holiness must be governed by Reason.   But so must Arthur.   In canto ix, in which Arthur tells of the vision which caused him to fall in love with Gloriana, and of his pursuit of Glory, Arthur says:

> But me had warnd old Timons wise behest,
> Those creeping flames by reason to subdew, etc.[5]

Here again Reason is the determiner of the mean in regard to Highmindedness, or love of honor.   Finally, even the Paynim Sansfoy apologizes for forgetting "the raines to hold of reasons rule."[6]

We come now to Temperance.   Everyone knows that Spenser develops this virtue and the virtues of all his other Books by showing their opposites and by presenting various phases of the virtue and of its opposites, and that he tends to make any given virtue all-inclusive.   From the book of any one of Spenser's virtues a good case could be made out for all the moral virtues.   But Spenser not only

---

[1] Stanza 5.   [2] Stanza 12.   [3] Stanza 41.   [4] Stanza 42.   [5] Stanza 9.   [6] I, iv, 41.

presents various phases of Temperance; he treats the same phases of Temperance that Aristotle treats. For example, outside of Temperance and Incontinence in the strict sense, the kinds of intemperance most emphasized by Aristotle are incontinence in regard to angry passion, incontinence in regard to honor, and incontinence in regard to wealth or gain. Aristotle specially and repeatedly mentions these as things in regard to which men may be incontinent in the broad sense. For instance, he says: "Men are called incontinent in respect of angry passion, honor, and gain."[1] Now these are the very kinds of intemperance which, outside of intemperance in the strict sense, Spenser presents most strongly. Angry passion Spenser exemplifies in Furor; in Phedon, who, "chawing vengeance,"[2] murders his sweetheart and his bosom friend, and is trying to murder his sweetheart's maid when he falls into the hands of Furor; and in Pyrochles, who "Furors chayne unbinds."[3] Incontinence in respect of honor Spenser exemplifies in "Vaine Braggadocchio."[4] He is one of Aristotle's "Conceited people," who, says Aristotle, "are foolish and ignorant of themselves and make themselves conspicuous by being so. . . . . They get themselves up in fine dresses, and pose for effect, and so on, and wish their good fortune to be known to all the world, and talk about themselves as if that were the road to honor."[5] Braggadocchio represents Conceit, or desire of honor by one who is unworthy of it, one of the opposites of Highmindedness, or right love of honor on a great scale. Again, one of the greatest of the temptations in Spenser's Cave of Mammon is Ambition, one of Aristotle's extremes in regard to ordinary honors. Incontinence in regard to wealth or gain is, of course, powerfully presented in Mammon, who tempts the Knight of Temperance in canto vii.

But, in addition to treating it as a kind of center surrounded by opposites, Spenser treats Temperance as a mean between extremes, emphasizes one extreme in particular, and makes Reason the determiner of the mean. In the first canto of his Book on Temperance he works out Aristotle's mean concerning Temperance. Although Aristotle holds that all the virtues are concerned with pleasure and pain, he gives peculiar emphasis to the relation of Temperance to

---

[1] *N. Eth.*, VII, ii. [2] II, iv, 29. [3] II, v, Arg. [4] II, iii, Arg. [5] *N. Eth.*, IV, ix.

pleasure and pain in his definition of the virtue. He says: "In respect of pleasures and pains, although not indeed of all pleasures and pains, and to a less extent in respect of pains than of pleasures, the mean state is Temperance."[1] Again, in connection with Incontinence, Aristotle gives an important place to the vice of Effeminacy. He says:

Of the characters which have been described the one [incontinence] is rather a kind of effeminacy; the other is licentiousness. The opposite of the incontinent character is the continent, and of the effeminate the steadfast; for steadfastness consists in holding out against pain, and continence in overcoming pleasure, and it is one thing to hold out, and another to overcome, as it is one thing to escape being beaten and another to win a victory. . . . . If a person gives way where people generally resist and are capable of resisting, he deserves to be called effeminate. . . . . It is only unpardonable where a person is mastered by things against which most people succeed in holding out, and is impotent to struggle against them, unless his impotence be due to hereditary constitution or to disease, as effeminacy is hereditary in the kings of Scythia, or as woman is naturally weaker than a man.

And he continues: "It is people of a quick and atrabilious temper whose incontinence is particularly apt to take the form of impetuosity; for the rapidity or the violence of their feeling prevents them from waiting for the guidance of reason."[2] Finally, Aristotle condemns suicide as Effeminacy: "For it is effeminacy to fly from troubles, nor does the suicide face death because it is noble, but because it is a refuge from evil."[3] In canto i of Spenser's Book on Temperance we have the story of Mordant and Amavia. Acrasia (Intemperance), a beautiful but wicked enchantress, entices Sir Mordant away from his wife and finally poisons him; and the wife, in a fit of grief, commits suicide. Sir Guyon (the Knight of Temperance) and his Palmer (Reason or Prudence), having learned the story from the expiring wife, stand looking at the two dead bodies. Sir Guyon, turning to his Palmer, says:

Old Syre
Behold the image of mortalitie,
And feeble nature cloth'd with fleshly tyre,
When raging passion with fierce tyrannie,
Robs *reason* of her due regalitie,

---

[1] *N. Eth.*, II. vii.   [2] *Ibid.*, VII. viii.   [3] *Ibid.*, III. xi.

> And makes it servant to her basest part:
> The *strong* it weakens with infirmitie,
> And with bold furie armes the *weakest* hart;
> The strong through *pleasure* soonest falles, the
> weake through *smart*.

Then Sir Guyon's Palmer (Reason) replies:

> But *temperance* (said he) with golden squire
> *Betwixt them both* can measure out a *meane*,
> Neither to melt in *pleasures* whot desire,
> Nor fry in hartlesse *griefe* and dolefull *teene*.
> Thrise happie man, who *fares them both atweene*.[1]

Thus the incontinent Sir Mordant and the effeminate Amavia meet disaster because they fail to take the mean which Reason dictates in regard to "pleasure" and "smart." It will be noted that Spenser follows Aristotle even in such details as showing that greater strength is required to overcome pleasure than to resist pain. The importance which Spenser attaches to the suicide described in the episode is indicated by the name Amavia (Love of Life). Love of Life effeminately gives way to pain. The lesson of this canto cannot possibly be called "only incidental"; for Sir Guyon's relation to Mordant and Amavia is one of the larger elements of the plot, and one of the few discussed in Spenser's letter to Raleigh. It is the fate of Mordant and Amavia at the hands of Acrasia (Intemperance) which causes Guyon, the Knight of Temperance, to enter upon his quest to bind Acrasia.

So much for canto i. In canto ii Spenser works out the mean in regard to Aristotelian Temperance in the strict, or particular, sense.[2] Here, to quote Spenser's argument to the canto, Sir Guyon is shown

> the face of golden Meane.
> Her sisters two Extremities
> strive her to banish cleane.

Reason is made the determiner of the mean.[3]

What we have said of Spenser's treatment of Temperance as a mean between extremes is hardly more than a beginning of what

---

[1] II, i, 57–58.

[2] With the episode of Guyon's visit to Medina cf. *N. Eth.*, II, vii; III, xiii; and VII, xi.

[3] See especially II, ii, 38. See also stanzas 15 and 17.

could be said if space permitted. See, for example, canto xii, which is a series of studies of the mean. The truth is that the whole Book is a study of the mean. Like Aristotle, Spenser puts the emphasis on the extreme of excess, not on that of deficiency. Again, we have mentioned only a few of the numerous instances in which Spenser makes Reason the determiner of the mean. See, for example, the author's comments in stanzas 1–2 of canto xi, in which Spenser lays down the general principle that Reason is the determiner of the mean in regard to Temperance. Another point is worth noting. Although Aristotle makes Reason the determiner of the mean in the case of each of the moral virtues, he gives peculiar emphasis to the rule of Reason in regard to Temperance. Accordingly, Spenser gives the greatest possible emphasis to the rule of reason in respect of Temperance. For example, Aristotle says in his discussion of Temperance: "As a child ought to live according to the direction of his tutor (παιδαγωγός) so ought the concupiscent element in man to live according to the reason."[1] And Spenser gives his Knight of Temperance a tutor, the black Palmer, who continually accompanies, instructs, and directs him, and whom his "pupil"[2] (Guyon) faithfully obeys. It is hardly necessary to add that Guyon's Palmer is Reason. If other proof than the allegory be needed that he is so, it may be found, for example, in II, i, 34; or in II, iv, 2; or in II, xii, 38.

Passing to Chastity, Book III, we find that Spenser again follows Aristotle's method of treating a virtue and his conception of what a virtue is. Even Chastity is presented as a mean between extremes. Moreover, the extremes themselves are Aristotelian.

There is a very close relation between Shame, or Chastity, and Temperance. Both Aristotle and Spenser make Temperance include sex morality. The extremes of Aristotelian Shame, or Modesty, in the strict sense, are Shamelessness and Licentiousness, on the one hand, and Bashfulness, lack of courteous bearing, on the other.[3] The extremes of Aristotelian Temperance, in the strict sense, are Licentiousness and Incontinence, on the one hand, and Insensibility, or Asceticism, on the other.[4] Now it will be remembered that

[1] *N. Eth.*, III, xv.
[2] II, viii, 7.
[3] *N. Eth.*, II, vii, and IV, xv; *Rhetoric*, II, vi, and II, xii–xiii.
[4] *N. Eth.*, II, vii; III, xiii–xv; VII, especially chap. xi.

Spenser in his discussion of Chastity draws not only upon Aristotle's discussion of Shame, or Modesty, but also upon that part of his discussion of Temperance which has to do with sex morality. Accordingly he makes the extremes of his virtue of Chastity the Aristotelian extremes of Shamelessness, Licentiousness, and Incontinence, on the one hand, and Discourtesy and Insensibility, or Asceticism, or Celibacy, on the other.

In the proem to the Book on Chastity, Spenser tells us that just as Gloriana represents the rule of Elizabeth, so Belphoebe represents "her rare chastity," and he makes the same point in his letter to Raleigh. In telling how Belphoebe cared for her "flower" of "chastity and virtue virginal," he indicates the extremes:

> That dainty Rose, the daughter of her Morne,
> More deare then life she tendered, whose flowre
> The girlond of her honour did adorne:
> Ne suffred she the *Middayes scorching powre*,
> Ne the *sharp Northerne wind* thereon to showre,
> But lapped up her silken leaves most chaire,
> When so the froward skye began to lowre:
> But soone as calmed was the Christall aire,
> She did it faire dispred, and let to florish faire.[1]

For the Courtesy of Belphoebe see, in III, v, 27–55,[2] the story of her nursing the wounded Timias and of her treatment of him, a social inferior, when he falls in love with her. Belphoebe is praised because she can be chaste without running into the extreme of Discourtesy:

> In so great prayse of stedfast *chastity*,
> *Nathlesse* she was so *curteous and kind*,
> Tempred with *grace* and goodly *modesty*,
> That seemed those *two vertues* strove to find
> The higher place in her Heroick mind.

To realize the seriousness of this extreme of Discourtesy it is only necessary to note the contemptible character of the discourteous Mirabella in Spenser's Book on Courtesy. Discourtesy here clearly includes the idea of celibacy. It should be remembered that Spenser's Courtesy is Aristotle's Friendliness—readiness to act as a true friend

[1] III, v, 51. See also stanzas 50–55, especially 52.
[2] Note especially III, v, 54–55. See also III, vi, 1–3.

would act—and that, with both Aristotle and Spenser, Friendship includes love. In his argument to canto vii of Book VI Spenser tells us that we are to learn of "Fayre Mirabellaes punishment for loves disdaine decreed." Mirabella is cruel to her lovers and even boasts of the fact that they suffer and die because of their love for her. "She did all love despize." She is determined to live a life of celibacy.

> She was borne free, not bound to any wight,
> And so would ever live, and love her owne delight.[1]

Such is the Discourtesy, or Unfriendliness, which is one of the extremes in regard to Chasity. Mirabella is finally brought to justice by Cupid.

Another passage in which Spenser represents Discourtesy and Celibacy as an extreme in regard to Chastity is in canto vi of the Book on Chastity. Venus has lost her little son, Cupid. In searching a wood for him, she comes upon her sister, Diana, of whom she makes inquiries. Diana is ungracious, intolerant:

> Thereat Diana gan to smile, in scorne
> Of her vaine plaint, and to her scoffing sayd;
> "Great pittie sure, that ye be so forlorne
> Of your gay sonne, that gives you so good ayd
> To your disports: ill mote ye bene apayd."
> But she was more engrieved, and replide;
> "Faire sister, ill beseemes it to upbrayd
> A dolefull heart with so disdainfull pride;
> The like that mine, may be your paine another tide.
>
> . . . .
>
> And ill becomes you with your loftie creasts,
> To scorne the joy, that Jove is glad to seek;
> We both are bound to follow heavens beheasts,
> And tend our charges with obeisance meeke.
> Spare, gentle sister, with reproch my paine to eeke."[2]

After Diana has made further insulting speeches, she is finally induced to join in the search for Cupid. While searching, Diana and Venus find Belphoebe and Amoretta, two babes born at a birth, Belphoebe being born first, and then Amoretta, to show that first comes maidenly chastity, "perfect Maydenhed," and then love and

---

[1] VI, vii, 30–31.   [2] III, vi, 21–22.

"goodly womanhed." Diana and Venus decide each to adopt one of the babes.

> Dame Phoebe [Diana] to a Nymph her babe betooke,
> To be upbrought in perfect Maydenhed,
> And to her selfe her name Belphoebe red:
> But Venus hers thence farre away convayed,
> To be upbrought in goodly womanhed.[1]

Venus takes Amoretta to be brought up in the Garden of Adonis, where, we are told,

> All things, as they created were, doe grow,
> And yet remember well *the mightie word,*
> *Which first was spoken by th' Almightie lord,*
> *That bad them to increase and multiply.*[2]

Perhaps Spenser's plainest condemnation of Celibacy and Insensibility, or Asceticism, is the episode dealing with Marinell in the Book on Chastity. Marinell is "a mighty man at arms." He eschews the love of women, for Proteus, the sea-god and prophet, has taught his mother to keep him from all womankind:

> For thy she gave him warning every day,
> The love of women not to entertaine;
> A lesson too too hard for living clay,
> From love in course of Nature to refraine:
> Yet he his mothers lore did well retaine,
> And ever from faire Ladies love did fly;
> Yet many Ladies fair did oft complaine,
> That they for love of him would algates dy:
> Dy, who so list for him, he was loves enimy.[3]

One of the first great victories of Britomart (Chastity) is her defeat of this sturdy champion.

Though Britomart leaves Marinell for dead, his mother, Cymoent, by her magic finally revives him. We now learn that fair Florimell loves Marinell, but is scorned by him. In canto xi of Book IV Spenser gives a synopsis of the story of Marinell and Florimell, in order to continue it. The lovely Florimell, because she will not grant her love to the sea-god Proteus, is suffering horrible torments at Proteus' hands.

> And all this was for love of Marinell,
> Who her despysed (ah who would her despyse?)
> And *wemens love did from his hart expell,*
> *And all those joyes that weak mankind entyse.*[4]

---

[1] III, vi, 28.   [2] III, vi, 34.   [3] III, iv, 25–26.   [4] IV, xi, 5.

Clearly this is Celibacy and Insensibility, or Asceticism. Marinell is finally reformed by the love of Florimell.

One more episode might be given here. It is in the opening canto of the Book on Chastity. Britomart, who fights for Chastity, and the Red Cross Knight (Holiness), who "gave her good aid," come in their journey to "Castle Joyous," presided over by the witch Malecasta, called "the Lady of Delight." In the "sumptuous guize" of Castle Joyous the knights see

> The image of superfluous riotize,
> Exceeding much the state of meane degree.[1]

Smith and Selincourt define the term "meane," in this passage, as "middling"; and indeed the context seems to make any other interpretation impossible.

Proof that the contemptible Mirabella of the Book on Courtesy is Discourtesy (if that can need special proof), and that Marinell of the Book on Chastity also illustrates Discourtesy—both being guilty of the serious offense of Cruelty, Unfriendliness, toward their lovers—may be had by comparing their conduct with the Courtesy of Britomart (Chastity) toward even the amorous "Lady of Delight," who, deceived by Britomart's armor, woos the Knight of Chastity in no modest manner. Britomart considers the feelings of other people and therefore does not rebuff the Lady of Delight until her conduct becomes outrageous:

> For thy she would not in discourteise wise,
> Scorne the faire offer of good will profest;
> For great rebuke it is, love to despise,
> Or rudely sdiegne a gentle harts request.[2]

Finally, a consideration of the characters in Book III shows plainly that Spenser treats Chastity as a mean, and that his extremes are the Aristotelian ones already mentioned. Marinell and Diana go to extremes in the direction of Discourtesy and Celibacy. Britomart, Belphoebe, Amoretta, and the true Florimell represent the mean. The extreme of Licentiousness is emphatically represented in the horrible Titan twins, Argante and Ollyphant, the hyena-like Brute, Proteus, Malecasta, the false Florimell, the infamous Hellenore, and Busyrane.

[1] III, i, 33.   [2] III, i, 55.

In addition to treating Chastity as a mean, Spenser not only discusses various phases of the virtue, after the manner of Aristotle, but draws from Aristotle the virtues and vices which he discusses in connection with Chastity. This fact throws light on an otherwise difficult passage in the *Faerie Queene*. In his continued discussion of Temperance,[1] already referred to, Aristotle has a curious discussion of brutality, or unnatural vice. "There is more excuse," he says, "for following natural impulses, as indeed there is for following all such desires as are common to all the world, and the more common they are, the more excusable they are also."[2] Again he says, "And if these are brutal states, there are others which are produced in some people by disease and madness. . . . . Other such states again are the result of a morbid disposition or of habit." In this brutal or unnatural conduct he includes "unnatural vice," which he elsewhere refers to as "unnatural passion."[3] Compare this with Book III, canto ii, of the *Faerie Queene*. Britomart, who represents Elizabeth as well as Chastity, is madly in love with Artegall (Justice). In the midst of this fine compliment to the Queen we have the following curious passage put in the mouth of Glauce, Britomart's old nurse, after Britomart has confessed her love:

> Daughter (said she) what need ye be dismayd,
> Or why make ye such Monster of your mind?
> *Of much more uncouth thing I was affrayd;*
> *Of filthy lust, contrarie unto kind:*
> But this affection nothing straunge I find;
> For who with *reason* can you aye reprove,
> To love the semblant pleasing most your mind,
> And yield your heart, whence ye cannot remove?
> No guilt in you, but in the tyranny of love.

> Not so th' Arabian Myrrhe did set her mind;
> Nor so did Biblis spend her pining hart,
> But lov'd their native flesh against all kind,
> And to their purpose used wicked art:
> Yet played Pasiphaë a more monstrous part,
> That lov'd a bull, and learned a beast to bee;
> Such *shamefull* lusts who loaths not, which depart
> From course of *nature* and of *modestie?*
> Sweet love such lewdness bands from his faire companie.[4]

---

[1] *N. Eth.*, VII, i and vi–vii. [2] *Ibid.*, VII, vii. [3] *Ibid.*, VII, vi. [4] III, ii, 40–41.

I cannot resist giving another example of Spenser's conformity to Aristotle's scheme. In cantos ix and x of Spenser's Book on Chastity we have the story of Hellenore and Malbecco. The latter, at first a real character, in canto x becomes Jealousy in one of the most powerful of all Spenser's personifications. It is the unlikeness of Malbecco and Hellenore which causes their great unhappiness. This unlikeness includes the fact that Malbecco has reached the age of impotence, while his wife is young. Their unhappiness results in the "rape" of Hellenore (Helen) by Paridell (Paris). That their unhappiness is brought about by their inequality and unlikeness is clear from reading the cantos. I quote a few passages, however, which establish this point by literal exposition:

> But all his mind is set on mucky pelfe,
> Yet is he lincked to a lovely lasse,
>
> . . . .
>
> The which to him both far unequall yeares,
> And also far unlike conditions has;
> For she does joy to play emongst her peares,
> And to be free from hard restraint and gealous feares.
>
> But he is old, and withered like hay,
> Unfit faire Ladies service to supply.
> The privie guilt whereof makes him alway
> Suspect her truth, and keepe continuall spy
> Upon her with his other blincked eye;
> Ne suffreth he resort of living wight
> Approch to her, ne keepe her company,
> But in close bowre her mewes from all mens sight,
> Depriv'd of kindly joy and naturall delight.
>
> Malbecco he, and Hellenore she hight,
> Unfitly yokt together in one teeme.
>
> . . . .
>
> Fast good will with gentle courtesyes,
> And timely service to her pleasures meet
> May her perhaps containe, that else would algates fleet.[1]

Now there is a very close relation between the virtues of Chastity and Friendship, for Aristotle makes Friendship include love and the relation of husband and wife.[2] Again, Aristotle repeatedly makes

[1] III, ix, 4–7.
[2] That Aristotelian Friendship includes love is clear from the whole of Book VIII of *N. Eth.* The Friendship of husband and wife is discussed specifically in chap. xii.

the point that perfect Friendship requires perfect equality and likeness, and that any Friendship requires approximate equality and
likeness. For example, he says: "In Friendship quantitative
equality is first and proportionate second. This is clearly seen to be
the case if there be a wide distinction between two persons in respect
of virtue, vice, affluence, or anything else. For persons so widely
different cease to be friends; they do not even affect to be friends."[1]
Thus the lesson that the inequality and unlikeness of Malbecco and
Hellenore is the cause of their destruction is straight Aristotelian
doctrine. But this is not all. In the *Politics*, which is a continua-
tion of the *Nicomachean Ethics*,[2] Aristotle discusses the subject of
marriage. At the beginning of chapter xvi of Book VI he says:

> In legislating about this association [marriage] he [the legislator] should
> have in view, not only the persons themselves who are to marry, but their
> time of life, so that they may arrive simultaneously at corresponding periods
> in respect of age, and there may not be a discrepancy between their powers,
> whether it is that the husband is still able to beget children and the wife
> is not, or *vice versa*, as this is a state of things which is a source of mutual
> bickerings and dissentions.

And Aristotle reiterates the idea throughout the chapter. That this
point is the part of the lesson to which Spenser gives emphasis is
clear, not only from the story and the literal exposition, but also
from the name Malbecco.[3] But even the idea of the impotent old
husband's love of money and disregard of honor is Aristotelian.
In the *Nicomachean Ethics*, IV, iii, Aristotle says: "Illiberality is
incurable; for it seems that old age or impotence of any kind makes
men illiberal," and he repeats this thought in the *Rhetoric*.[4]

Again, Spenser makes it indisputably clear that reason is the
determiner of the right course in respect of Chastity. Thus, as we
have already seen, the old nurse Glauce, who in a measure represents
Reason, or Prudence, assures Britomart (Chastity) that her conduct

---

[1] *N. Eth.*, VIII, ix.

[2] Not only the last chapter of the *N. Eth.* but the whole book prepares the way for
the *Politics*. It is upon the relation between Morality and Reason, or Prudence, explained
n the *N. Eth.*, that the legislator of the *Politics* bases his laws.

[3] Ital. *becco*, a buck, a goat, a cuckold; cf. Marston, *Malcontent*, I, i, 118–20:
M. Duke, thou art a *becco*, a cornuto.
P. How?
M. Thou art a cuckold.

[4] II, xiii.

is right, for it is in accordance with Reason.[1] On the other hand, we are told concerning the unholy passion of the witch's son:

> So strong is passion that no *reason* hears.[2]

In discussing the virtue of Friendship, Spenser does not make much of the mean. But neither does his master. Aristotle only suggests that perhaps we ought to observe the mean in regard to the number of friendships which we undertake to maintain. Like Aristotle, however, Spenser does develop the virtue of Friendship by showing its opposites and by presenting various phases of the virtue and of its opposites. Thus he discusses Discord as well as Concord, Hate as well as Love,[3] Falseness (Duessa) as well as "Friendship trew." He shows not only the friendship of the virtuous, as seen in such cases as that of Cambel and Triamond, but also the friendship of the vicious, friendship for gain, and so on, in such cases as the friendship of Blandamour and Paridell, which, in accordance with Aristotle's teaching, soon ends in strife.[4] Professor Erskine[5] asserts that Spenser's Book on Friendship "seems at first sight to treat only of jealousies and quarrels." He brings forward *two sentences* of Cicero from which he thinks Spenser must have learned that it was possible to present Friendship by showing its opposite. The fact is that in presenting Friendship by showing its opposite Spenser is not only doing what Aristotle did in everyone of his virtues, but is doing what he himself did in every book of the *Faerie Queene*.

Moreover, Spenser discusses the same opposites and phases of Friendship that Aristotle discusses. For example, Aristotle deals with the friendship of the virtuous, which endures, and the friendship of the vicious, friendship for gain, and so on, which does not endure. We have already seen that Spenser represents these phases of Friendship. Again, Aristotle's Friendship is of three main kinds: the friendship of kinsmen, the friendship of love, including marriage, and friendship in the ordinary sense.[6] In IV, ix, 1–3 of the *Faerie Queene*, Spenser gives a plain, literal exposition of these three kinds

---

[1] III, ii, 40.
[2] III, vii, 21.
[3] IV, x, 34 and 32.
[4] IV, ii, 13, 18.
[5] *Pub. Mod. Lang. Assoc.*, XXIII, 846.
[6] See, for example, *N. Eth.*, VIII, xii.

of Friendship, as Professor Erskine has observed;[1] and he reiterates this classification throughout the book.[2] Again, in connection with love Spenser illustrates the Aristotelian extremes of insensibility, or celibacy, unreasonable love, inconstancy, and licentiousness.[3] Once more, in the Book on Friendship, as well as in the Book on Chastity, Spenser follows Aristotle in making equality and likeness essential to Friendship. Friendship is impossible between Cambell and any one of the three brothers, Priamond, Diamond, and Triamond.[4] But when Triamond, by receiving the spirits of his two brothers, becomes the equal of Cambell, the two become perfect friends.[5] Spenser does not stop, however, at showing friendship between these equals of high degree; he shows also friendship between two equal and like persons of low degree, the two squires in cantos viii and ix.[6] Finally, the most striking thing about Aristotle's discussion of Friendship is his identification of this virtue with Concord in the State. He says: "Again, it seems that friendship or love is the bond which holds states together, and that legislators set more store by it than by justice; for concord is apparently akin to friendship, and it is concord that they especially seek to promote, and faction, as being hostility to the state, that they especially try to expel."[7] Even this phase of Aristotelian Friendship is emphatically presented in the *Faerie Queene*. In the first canto of his Book on Friendship Spenser presents Discord, the enemy of Friendship, whom the wicked witch Duessa has brought from hell "to trouble noble knights."

> Her name was Ate, mother of *debate*,
> And all *dissention* which doth dayly grow
> Amongst fraile men, that many a *publike state*
> And many a *private* oft doth overthrow.
>
> . . . .
> Hard by the gates of hell her dwelling is,
>
> . . . .
> Yet many waies to enter may be found,

---

[1] *Pub. Mod. Lang. Assoc.*, XXIII, 849.

[2] Note, for example, the "friends," "brethren," and "lovers" of IV, i, 24.

[3] See IV, ix, 21.

[4] IV, ii–iii.

[5] IV, iii, 26–37, especially 37.

[6] See especially viii, 55–56, and ix, 10–11.

[7] *N. Eth.*, VIII, i.

> But none to issue forth when one is in:
> For *discord* harder is to end then to begin.

> And all within the riven walls were hung
> With ragged monuments of times forepast,
> All which the sad effects of *discord* sung.

Among these "monuments" are "broken scepters," "great cities ransackt," and "nations captived and huge armies slaine." "There was the signe of antique Babylon," of Thebes, of Rome, of Salem, and "sad Ilion." There were the names of Nimrod and "of Alexander, and his Princes five Which shar'd to them the spoiles that he had got alive." And there too were the "relicks . . . . of the dreadfull *discord*, which did drive The noble Argonauts to outrage fell."

> For all this worlds faire workmanship she tride,
> Unto his last confusion to bring,
> And that great golden chaine quite to divide,
> With which it blessed *Concord* hath together tide.

Thus Spenser follows Aristotle in making Friendship include Concord in the State. The same idea comes out in Spenser's presentation of Concord in canto x:

> *Concord* she cleeped was in common reed,
> Mother of blessed *Peace*, and Friendship trew.[1]

In discussing his fifth virtue, Justice, Spenser expresses the mean in almost the exact words of Aristotle. Aristotle tells us that particular Justice has to do with the goods of fortune.[2] He defines Justice as follows: "Just conduct is a mean between committing and suffering injustice; for to commit injustice is to have too much, and to suffer it is to have too little."[3] In the proem to Book V Spenser in describing the Golden Age, when all men were just, says:

> And all men sought their owne, and none no more.

Again, in Book V proper, Spenser's treatment of Justice as a mean is unmistakable. In canto ii we have the Gyant with his "huge great paire of ballance." Complaining that this world's goods are unjustly, because unequally, distributed, the Gyant proposes to weigh everything and make a just distribution. He has asserted

---

[1] *IV, x, 34.*   [2] *N. Eth.,* V, ii.   [3] *N. Eth.,* V, ix.

that he "could *justly* weigh the *wrong and right*," and Artegall (Justice) is testing him. Artegall finally tells him:

> But set the truth and set the right aside,
> For they with wrong or falshood will not fare;
> And put *two wrongs* together to be tride,
> Or else *two falses*, each of equall share;
> And then together doe them both compare.
> For truth is one, and right is ever one.
> So did he, and then plaine it did appeare,
> Whether of them the greater were attone.
> *But right sate in the middest of the beame alone.*
>
> But he the right from thence did thrust away,
> For it was not the right, which he did seeke;
> But rather strove extremities to way,
> Th' one to diminish th' other for to eeke.
> For of the meane he greatly did misleeke.[1]

At this point Talus, Artegall's iron squire (the iron hand of Justice), hurls the Gyant into the sea and drowns him. This mean which the Gyant "misleekes," and which Justice demands, is not simply a mean, but Aristotle's mean of Justice; for it is the mean in regard to the distribution of the goods of fortune. Moreover, the episode is Aristotelian in every particular. Aristotle teaches that equality as applied to Justice must be proportionate, not absolute. Justice, he holds, demands that the goods of fortune be distributed proportionately to the varying degrees of virtue in the citizens.[2] He even protests particularly against an equalization of property and reiterates this protest.[3]

Spenser's characters in this Book represent not only the mean but also the two Aristotelian extremes in regard to Justice: that of accepting less than rightfully belongs to one, and that of taking more. The first is represented by the Squire who is wronged by Sir Sanglier. Sanglier will not "rest contented with his right,"[4] but, "the fairere love to gaine," takes the Squire's Ladie and slays

[1] V, ii, 45–49.
[2] *N. Eth.*, Book V. Aristotle makes the same point in his discussion of Friendship. See *N. Eth.*, VIII, ix.
[3] See, for example, *Politics*, VIII, ix.
[4] V, i, 17.

his own. The Squire complains to Artegall. Brought before Artegall for judgment, Sanglier defies his accuser, and testifies falsely that—

> neither he did shed that Ladies bloud
> Nor tooke away his love, but *his owne proper good.*

Then

> Well did the Squire perceive himself too weake,
> To aunswere his defiaunce in the field,
> And rather chose his challenge off to breake,
> Then to approve his right with speare and shield.
> And rather guilty chose him selfe to yield.[1]

Only by imitating Solomon is Artegall able to discover to whom the live Ladie belongs and who is the murderer. The other extreme is represented by Sanglier, the robber Pollente, his daughter Munera, the Gyant with the huge "ballance," and so on. Like Aristotle, Spenser puts the emphasis on the extreme of taking too much. The opposite of general Justice is represented by such characters as Grantorto (Great Wrong). The mean is seen in Artegall, Arthur, Britomart, and Mercilla (Equity).

The various phases of Justice discussed by Aristotle are clearly presented by Spenser, such as distributive justice, corrective justice, retaliation, equity, and so on. Spenser also plainly makes Reason the determiner of the mean in respect to Justice. See, for example, his literal exposition of Justice in V, ix, 1 ff.

Spenser's sixth virtue, Courtesy, is not only treated as a mean, but is exactly Aristotle's mean in regard to Friendliness. As we have already seen, Aristotle makes Friendliness consist in acting as a true friend would act.[2] He makes its extremes Surliness, Contentiousness, Unfriendliness, on the one hand, and Flattery and Obsequiousness, or Complaisance, on the other. His friendly man is pleasant to live with, for he is free from Surliness or Contentiousness; but he will not yield his approval or withhold his condemnation when wrong conduct is under consideration. This is why he is like a true friend. Here we have exactly the character of Spenser's Knight of Courtesy, as is shown, for example, by Spenser's literal exposition of Sir Calidore's Courtesy, in VI, i, 2–3. It is plain that the Blatant Beast,

---

[1] V, i, 23, 24.   [2] *N. Eth.*, IV, xii.

⁄hich Calidore, the Knight of Courtesy, is to bind, is one extreme in regard to Courtesy. Blandina[1] represents the opposite extreme. Calidore is, of course, the mean. Clearly Spenser puts the emphasis on Surliness, Contentiousness. We have already seen that Spenser develops the virtue of Courtesy by showing its opposites and by presenting various phases of the virtue and of its opposites. Further, that Reason is the determiner of the right course in regard to this virtue Spenser repeatedly makes clear. Enias, for example, appeals to Arthur, who here represents Courtesy, to rescue—

> Yond Lady and her Squire with foule despight
> Abusde, against all *reason* and all law.[2]

Thus I have shown, beyond question, I hope, that Spenser follows Aristotle in essentials. Incidentally many correspondences in details have been pointed out, but lack of space makes it impossible to show how numerous such correspondences are.

At one point Spenser interprets his Aristotle with considerable freedom. He assigns Magnificence to Arthur, "which vertue," he says, "for that (according to Aristotle and the rest) it is the perfection of all the rest, and containeth in it them all," etc.[3] Jusserand, conceiving that there is no warrant in Aristotle for any such statement, says, "He follows here, as a matter of fact, neither Aristotle nor the rest."[4] Jusserand sees in Spenser's statement evidence that the poet's recollection of Aristotle was vague, and he finally intimates—what Professor Erskine, following him, states—that Spenser probably never had read Aristotle's *Ethics*.

Now suppose we could demonstrate that Spenser's memory did fail him at this point, that he actually was confused as to the Aristotelian meaning of Magnificence ($\mu\epsilon\gamma\alpha\lambda o\pi\rho\epsilon\pi\epsilon\iota\alpha$). The fact would prove little. Greene,[5] Herford,[6] and others have proved that Spenser more than once forgot the thread of his own story in the *Faerie Queene*. If a slip in memory is evidence that Spenser knew little of, and had probably never read, Aristotle's *Ethics*, there is equal

[1] See especially VI, vi, 41–42.
[2] VI, viii, 6; see also VI, iii, 49.
[3] Letter to Sir Walter Raleigh.
[4] *Mod. Phil.*, III, 382.
[5] *Pub. Mod. Lang. Assoc.*, IV, 173 ff.
[6] See Professor Child's edition of Spenser's poems, note to I, i, 52.

evidence that he knew little of, and had probably never read, the *Faerie Queene*. But there is no evidence that Spenser's memory did fail him at this point; and there is much evidence that it did not.

Let us see what authority exists in Aristotle for Spenser's assignment of Magnificence to the morally perfect Arthur. First we must decide what is Aristotle. Jusserand says: "Three treatises on morals have come down to us under the name of Aristotle; one alone, the *Nicomachean Ethics*, being, as it seems, truly his; the others appear to be a make-up, drawn from his teachings by some disciples."[1] This is a kind of *ex post facto* judgment. Friedrich D. E. Schleiermacher, the great critic and Aristotelian scholar, born one hundred and seventy years after Spenser's death, held that the *Magna Moralia* was the source of the *Nicomachean Ethics* and of the *Eudemian Ethics*.[2] Only recently have scholars begun to agree that the *Nicomachean Ethics* is probably the most truly Aristotelian of the three. An uncritical scholar like Spenser would certainly have made no such distinction. He would simply have accepted all three as the teachings of Aristotle, as they really are.

There is ample warrant in Aristotle for the idea that one of the moral virtues may be thought of as containing all the others. For example, it is clear from the *Nicomachean Ethics* that Magnanimity (I have elsewhere used the term Highmindedness) would fill this requirement;[3] for although Magnanimity, or Highmindedness, is essentially love of great honor, it includes moral perfection in the fullest sense. Again, on the same authority Justice, in the broad sense, includes all the moral virtues so far as one's relations to others are concerned. But under Spenser's plan, set forth in the letter to Raleigh, the virtue assigned to Arthur could have no Book; and Spenser was too much interested in church matters and in politics not to write on Holiness and Justice. Besides, there would be a kind of impropriety in omitting the former; probably the Scripture text "Seek ye first the Kingdom of God and His righteousness; and all these things shall be added unto you" had something to do, not only with Spenser's writing on Holiness, but also with his treating it

---

[1] *Mod. Phil.*, III, 374.

[2] *The Works of Aristotle, Translated into English under the Editorship of W. D. Ross: Magna Moralia, Ethica Eudemia, De Virtutibus et Vitiis* (Oxford, 1915), Introd., p. v.

[3] *N. Eth.*, IV, vii, and II, vii.

first. It was highly desirable then to reserve Highmindedness, or Magnanimity, and Justice for what we know as the First and Fifth Books. (If, as Jusserand holds, Spenser had already written the Book on Holiness when he completed the plan set forth in his letter to Raleigh, it was absolutely necessary to leave Highmindedness, Magnanimity, as the virtue of the Knight of Holiness; for it would do admirably for him, and no other virtue would do.) Thus if Spenser could assign some other virtue to Arthur, he could make the plan of his poem more elastic.

Now there was another virtue which was peculiarly adapted to Arthur, provided it could be made to include all the virtues—namely, Magnificence. According to the *Nicomachean Ethics*, "Magnificence is suitable to . . . . persons of rank and reputation and the like, as all these advantages confer importance and dignity."[1] Rank? Arthur's was the highest. Reputation? Spenser tells us in the letter to Raleigh that it was because of Arthur's reputation that he chose him as the hero of the *Faerie Queene*, he "being made famous by many men's former works." Again, the magnificent man labors for the public good and strives for honor. Once more, "The motive of the magnificent man in incurring expense will be nobleness; for nobleness is a characteristic of all the virtues." "In a word, Magnificence is excellence of work on a great scale."[2] What could better describe Arthur's great works?

But can Magnificence be made to include all the virtues? Although in a strict sense it is simply a mean between meanness and vulgar display in the use of money, it seems to include much more. Moreover, there is, as we have already seen, abundant authority in the *Nicomachean Ethics* for taking the virtues not only in a strict but also in a broad or metaphorical sense. If Magnificence were similarly interpreted, it would be "the perfection of all the rest and contain in it them all." But all this is from the *Nicomachean Ethics*. What do Aristotle's other works on morals say about Magnificence? The *Magna Moralia* says: "But there are, as people think, more kinds of Magnificence than one; for instance, people say, 'His walk was Magnificent,' and there are of course other uses of the term

[1] IV, iv; II, vii.

[2] Cf. Aristotle's discussion of the magnificent man, *N. Eth.*, IV, iv–v.

Magnificent in a metaphorical, not in a strict, sense."[1] This is certainly suggestive. And according to the *Ethica Eudemia*, "The magnificent man is not concerned with any and every action or choice, but with expenditure—unless we use the term metaphorically."[2] Here is a plain suggestion that Magnificence could be taken in a broad sense, could be made to include "any and every action or choice." Such is Magnificence, "according to Aristotle." Who "the rest" are is not quite clear, but Spenser's favorite poet, Chaucer, says in his *Persones Tale*, "Thanne comth Magnificence, that is to seyn, whan a man dooth and perfourneth grete werkes of goodnesse"[3] —exactly what Arthur "dooth."

We come now to Jusserand's third and last main argument. Jusserand contends that Spenser did not get his virtues from Aristotle and proceeds to argue that he did get them from his friend Lodowick Bryskett, and from Piccolomini's *Istitutione morale*, through Bryskett. He thus finds it necessary to get over Spenser's own assertion that he did take his virtues from Aristotle. He argues that "Spenser showed as a rule no minute accuracy in his indications of sources and models, and he did not display more than usual in this particular case."[4] The first part of the proposition is true. But to find that "as a rule" Spenser showed no "minute accuracy" is a vastly different thing from concluding that a solemn statement concerning the substance of his whole *Faerie Queene* is "misleading, every word of it."

Let us examine Jusserand's argument[5] that Spenser derived his virtues from Bryskett, and from Piccolomini through Bryskett. Long after Spenser's death Bryskett published *A Discourse of Civil Life*,[6] a translation from Giraldi Cinthio's three dialogues *Dell' allevare et ammaestrare i figluoli nella vita civile*. It is an account of the best way to *rear children* and includes a discussion of moral virtues in which the number twelve is mentioned. That Spenser knew this *Discourse* Jusserand concludes from the fact that Bryskett represents Spenser as one of the interlocutors in the conversation which furnishes the machinery of the book. Before the day of Spenser and Bryskett,

---

1 I. xxvi.
2 III. vi.
3 736 (§ 61).

4 *Mod. Phil.*, III, 374.
5 *Ibid.*, III, 378–80.
6 London. 1606.

Piccolomini, taking Aristotle and Plato as his masters, had written his *Istitutione morale*, in which he discussed eleven moral virtues and added the statement that Prudence, which he classed as an intellectual virtue, might be considered a moral virtue. Jusserand holds that "twelve was a kind of sacred number and was sure to come in." In his *Discourse* Bryskett states that when he came to the question of the moral virtues he found that Cinthio had treated them "somewhat too briefly and confusedly," and adds, "I have therefore, to help mine own understanding, had recourse to Piccolomini."[1] Jusserand takes this statement as "positive testimony" that Spenser knew the substance of the *Istitutione morale*. Jusserand concludes: "From such books and such *conversations*, from other less solemn *talks* which he and Bryskett, interested in the same problems, could not fail to have, Spenser derived his *list of virtues* and his *ideas regarding a list of twelve*."

Now it is quite possible that Spenser, the genius, should get his ideas from Lodowick Bryskett, a man of no great parts. It is also possible, however improbable, that Spenser read Bryskett's book twenty years before it was published. But there is no proof, or even evidence, that such was the case. And, by the same token, there is no evidence that Spenser knew Piccolomini's *Istitutione*. Professor Erskine has proved, what most careful students must already have suspected, that Bryskett's "conversation" which furnishes Jusserand's "positive testimony" is a myth. In putting his discussion into the form of a dialogue in which he himself, Spenser, the Bishop of Armagh, and others are the speakers, Bryskett is simply following a literary convention of the day. It is impossible to suppose all the characters of the dialogue actually together at Bryskett's cottage.[2] Besides, Erskine finds that the speeches which Bryskett puts into the mouths of Spenser and the good Bishop of Armagh are translated straight from Giraldi Cinthio. He finds further that even if the dialogue had been a real one it could have had little to do with Piccolomini, for it contains only one passage from him. It may be added that Bryskett could have taken the idea for the machinery of his *Discourse* from Spenser's *Mother Hubberds Tale*. In both cases

---

[1] *Mod. Phil.*, III, 378–80.

[2] *Pub. Mod. Lang. Assoc.*, XXIII, 831–50.

the author is sick, his friends come in to see him, and the conversation which is later given to the reader takes place. The only difference is that Bryskett is so anxious to take the credit of authorship that he commits the absurdity of having the sick man, Bryskett himself, do the talking, which consists in lecturing on philosophy for three days.

In the next place, even if Spenser had known Bryskett's *Discourse*, he could not have taken his virtues and the plan of his *Faerie Queene* from it. For one reason, Spenser's and Bryskett's virtues are unlike in nature. For example, Bryskett, like Plato, makes Prudence one of the moral virtues, whereas Spenser, as we have already seen, follows Aristotle in making it that intellectual virtue which determines the mean in the case of each of the moral virtues. Again, Bryskett makes Magnanimity a subordinate virtue, whereas Spenser, like Aristotle, makes it include all the moral virtues. Moreover, Spenser's basis of classification is quite different from Bryskett's. In Bryskett's classification, to quote his own words, "There are . . . . four principall vertues . . . . from which four are also derived (as branches from their trees) sundry others to make up the number twelve,"[1] whereas Spenser, like Aristotle, makes one of his virtues include all the others. Finally, even the agreement in point of number, which Jusserand would make much of, does not exist. Bryskett's number is twelve, Spenser's thirteen. And Spenser's plan of his poem, set forth in the letter to Raleigh, would have been impossible with any other number of virtues than thirteen. Thus it is plain that Spenser did not get his virtues from Bryskett.

[1] Quoted by Jusserand, *Mod. Phil.*, III, 380.

"MUTABILITY"

Little is known of the history of the fragment called "Mutability." The fragment was first published in 1609, ten years after the poet's death. It then appeared under the following title, which all editors have retained: "*Two Cantos of Mutability:* Which, both for Forme and Matter, appeare to be parcell of some following Booke of the *Faerie Queene,* under the legend of Constansie. Never before imprinted." Not another word of explanation was given.

The fragment has been a puzzle to editors. Dr. Grosart in his biography of Spenser, Volume I of his nine-volume edition of Spenser's works, speaks of it as "fragments" which show that Spenser had started on a "second six" books, to round out the proposed twelve. Thus he makes it a part of the *Faerie Queene,* and seems to expect to find other fragments. But by the time he has reached Volume VIII of his massive edition, and is ready to print the fragment, he has changed his mind. He now prefixes to the *Two Cantos on Mutability* the following note:

It is doubtful whether they were meant to form part of the *Faery Queene.* They make a charming independent poem on "Mutability"—one of Spenser's favorite themes.

Professor Child contents himself with printing them under the heading, "Book VII (?)." The Oxford edition disposes of the whole matter in a single sentence. It says simply: "The fragmentary Book VII appeared first in the Folio of 1609." Professor Dodge says that the best reason for thinking that the fragment was intended to form part of the *Faerie Queene* is found in stanza 37 of the first of the "Two Cantos."[1]

Besides the matter of its relation to Aristotle, there are, then, other interesting questions connected with "Mutability." Was it written as an independent poem? If not, where does it belong? Was it intended to be a part of the *Faerie Queene?*

It is hard to believe that "Mutability" was written as an independent poem. It is a unit, a great poem, in itself, as everyone must

[1] Cambridge ed., 1908, p. 131.

49

observe. But it is the two stanzas of canto viii that complete it. And these could easily have been added after the fragment was detached from the poem for which it was originally intended. Or they may well have been a part of the fragment; for they are in accord with Spenser's usual practice in the *Faerie Queene*, of beginning a canto with reflections on the preceding one. One reason for regarding "Mutability" as a fragment is the numbering of the cantos. If it was written as an independent poem, why the numbering as we have it—"Canto VI," "Canto VII," "The VIII. Canto, unperfite"? Closely connected with this is the presence of the proems which introduce cantos vi and vii. Surely these features are not the work of the printer. Again, a sufficient reason for doubting that what we have here was written as an independent poem is the fact that Spenser tells us in "Mutability," vi, 37, that this is part of a poem dealing with "warres and Knights," and in the part that we have no knights appear.

It seems clear that "Mutability" is part of an epic. Stanza 37 of canto vi, especially when compared with *Faerie Queene*, I, Prol. 1, can hardly leave a doubt on this point. The stanzas are as follows:

"Mutability," vi, 37:

> And, were it not ill fitting for this file,
> To sing of hilles and woods, mongst *warres and Knights*,
> I would abate the *sternenesse* of my stile,
> Mongst these *sterne* stounds to mingle soft delights;
> And tell how Arlo through Dianaes spights
> (Being of old the best and fairest Hill
> That was in all this holy Islands hights)
> Was made the most unpleasant, and most ill.
> Meane while, O Clio, lend Calliope thy quill.

Faerie Queene, I, Prol. 1:

> Lo I the man, whose Muse whilome did maske,
> As *time* her taught, in lowly Shepheards weeds,
> Am now enforst a far unfitter task,
> For trumpets *sterne* to chaunge mine Oaten reeds,
> And sing of *Knights* and Ladies gentle deeds;
> Whose prayses having slept in silence long,
> Me, all too meane, the sacred Muse areeds
> To blazon broad emongst her learned throng:
> Fierce *warres* and faithfull loves shall moralize my song.

Note that in "Mutability," vi, 37, Spenser not only shows that what
he is now writing is part of a poem dealing with "warres and Knights,"
but he speaks of the "sternenesse" of his present "stile" and of
"these sterne stounds," just as in *Faerie Queene*, I, Prol. 1, where
he is passing from his pastoral *Shepheardes Calender* to his epic
Faerie Queene, he speaks of changing his "Oaten reeds" for "trumpets
sterne." Again, in "Mutability," vi, 37, besides the mention of the
sternness of his epic style, Spenser gives unmistakable testimony
that he is here writing epic poetry. Wishing "mongst these sterne
stounds" to tell the story of how Arlo became cursed, the poet
prays Clio, the muse of history, to lend her quill to Calliope, the
muse of epic poetry. It is therefore clear that what has been written
up to this point is conceived as epic poetry—the work of Calliope.

If, then, "Mutability" was written as part of an epic poem, does
it belong to the *Faerie Queene* or to some other epic? First, what
do we know of Spenser's plans for writing epic poetry? We know,
from the famous letter to Raleigh, that Spenser had planned to write
six more books on moral virtues. There were to be twelve books in
the first part of *Faerie Queene*. We know, too, from the same source,
that, besides "these first twelve books," Spenser had it in mind to
write an "other part" to the *Faerie Queene*, which probably would
have been twelve books in length, making twenty-four books in the
completed *Faerie Queene*. This "other part" was to be on political
virtues.

In addition to the plans set forth in the letter to Raleigh, Spenser
makes certain other references to epic poetry which he intends to
write. Professor Child has pointed out that "Spenser once or twice
gives intimation of a purpose of commemorating the wars between
the Faerie Queene and the Paynim King, that is, Queen Elizabeth
and Philip of Spain." He cites the *Faerie Queene*, I, xi, 7, and I,
xii, 18, and Spenser's verses to the Earl of Essex, prefixed to the
Faerie Queene, and adds: "This intention, however, was never fully
carried out: all that the poet wrote upon the subject will be found in
the last cantos of the fifth book."[1] But in these passages Spenser
seems to be thinking of a discussion which he expects to introduce
somewhere in the *Faerie Queene*, perhaps in Book V, perhaps in

[1] *The Political Works of Edmund Spenser* (in *British Poets*), I (1855), 231.

Book XII, possibly in the Second Part, which is to deal with political virtues. The following line from the verses to Essex would seem to indicate a position at the close of the *Faerie Queene:* "To the last praises of this Faerie Queene." So far as we know, Spenser had no other epic poetry, than what we have mentioned, in mind or under way.

Apparently, then, "Mutability" was written as a part of the *Faerie Queene*, either of "these first twelve bookes" or of "the other part." And there are several additional facts which make this conclusion probable. The fragment is in the form of the *Faerie Queene*. It is divided into cantos like the *Faerie Queene*. The cantos are summarized in a proem, as is the case in the *Faerie Queene*. And the stanza form is that of the *Faerie Queene*. Again, a comparison of "Mutability," vi, 37, and *Faerie Queene*, I, Prol. 1, already quoted, indicates that the fragment was written as a part of the *Faerie Queene*. Note in both passages the reference to *knights*, "warres," and the sternness of style demanded by epic poetry. Spenser's usual meaning for the word "warres" is combats between two or more knights.[1] Furthermore, all the characters of the fragment are frequently mentioned in the *Faerie Queene*. Even its personification of rivers is a theme which is dwelt on at length in the *Faerie Queene*.[2] And the "records" of Mutability's "antique race and linage ancient" are found registered "in Faery Land."[3]

Seeing that "Mutability" was probably written to occupy some place in the *Faerie Queene*, one cannot refrain from asking, Where? This question is more difficult than the preceding ones. Realizing that the known facts are insufficient for a conclusive answer, one may nevertheless suggest a probable explanation.

The fragment may be, not, as the printer guessed, "parcell of some following Booke of the *Faerie Queene*," but rejected cantos from a preceding book. The fact that it is the middle of a book, not the beginning, as is shown by the numbering of the cantos, suggests this. It is improbable that any such vast amount of Spenser's poetry was lost as would be represented by five cantos of the *Faerie*

---

[1] See, for example, *F.Q.*, V, ii, 17.

[2] IV, xi.

[3] "Mutability," vi, 2.

Queene, or five such cantos as the two we have in the fragment—some twenty-seven-hundred verses. And it is improbable that Spenser would begin a book in the middle. If it were his practice to outline a book in detail before writing *in extenso,* he might be moved to develop a topic in the middle or at the end of a book before he had developed the beginning, and he would, of course, be able to assign the proper number to each canto. But there is no evidence that that was his practice; and there is evidence, both internal and external, that it was not. Professor Erskine, basing his reasoning on Books III and IV and Spenser's letter to Raleigh, has pointed out that Spenser could have had no outline of Book IV at the time when the first three books were published.[1] But there are other reasons for thinking that the fragment is rejected cantos from a preceding book. Change, or Fortune, was a favorite theme with Spenser. In whatever he wrote he could be counted on to discuss Change. We do not have to argue as to whether he could have put a discussion of Change in any one of Books I–VI; he *did* put it in, most notably in Books III and V. It would be easy for him in any of his books to launch into a long discussion of Change.

Before attempting to see whether the fragment would fit in some one of the completed books of the *Faerie Queene,* we should observe, however, that Spenser would not be likely to remove so great a portion of a book as is represented by the fragment without making some changes in what preceded and followed the rejected portion. It is conceivable that the fragment was part of a first draft of some book the remainder of which was reworked and given to us. A reason for rejection might be the great length to which the fragment runs without carrying on any thread of the story of the *Faerie Queene.* There are digressions in Books II and IV which are nearly a canto in length, or half as long as the fragment; but Guyon and Arthur read the long chronicles, and Marinell and his mother are present at the marriage of the Medway and the Thames. Again, the fragment might be rejected on the basis of tact or patriotism, as we shall see later. Finally, the fact that they are a unit in themselves, suitable to be published as a separate poem, would make rejection easy.

[1] *Pub. Mod. Lang. Assoc.,* XXIII, 831–50.

How would the fragment fit in Book II, Spenser's discussion of Temperance? It will be remembered that the fragment is divided into "Canto VI," "Canto VII," and "The VIII. Canto, unperfite." How would these cantos fit between canto v of Book II and what is now canto vi of Book II? At the close of II, v, Cymochles (Incontinence) has been roused by Atin from his bed of lust and led to avenge his brother Pyrochles' defeat and apparent death at the hands of Sir Guyon, the Knight of Temperance. He rides forth determined "to beene avenged that day" on Sir Guyon. He is impatient to avenge the defeat of his brother.[1] So ends canto v. In II, vi, Cymochles meets the beautiful Phaedria (Temptation to Incontinence) before he reaches Sir Guyon. He is easily led by Phaedria through the Lake of Idleness to her *wandering* island (Incontinence), where he forgets all about his purpose to avenge his brother's death. It would seem that between Cymochles' determination to avenge the defeat 'of his brother and his being led into Incontinence in which he forgets all about his brother—here it would seem that the fragment would fit neatly. It is Spenser's practice to begin a canto with reflections on what has passed, in the story, and what is to follow. Once launched into a discussion of Change, or Constancy, he might be led to pursue the subject to some definite stopping-place. It would be in accord with Spenser's practice to drop the story of Cymochles for a long time. He might not realize until later that he had here carried on no thread of the story of the *Faerie Queene*.

Would the fragment fit in Book III? There is a curious resemblance between the material of cantos vi–vii of the fragment and that of cantos vi–vii of Book III. In III, vi–vii, we have Diana and Belphoebe, who, as we know from the letter to Raleigh, represent Chastity and Elizabeth. In the fragment, vi–vii, we have the moon-goddess Diana, or Cynthia, or Phoebe, whose throne is attacked by Mutability. Besides the moon-goddess Diana, we have in the fragment a nineteen-stanza account of Diana as a virgin huntress. The privacy of her bath is invaded by the licentious Faunus, for which Faunus is punished and the country cursed. Again, in III,

---

[1] II. v. 38.

vi–vii, we have not only a discussion of Change, but a development of the idea that Change is in a Cycle, and that essentially there is no Change. The fragment, vi–vii, consists of a discussion of Change as a Cycle, and the same conclusion is reached as in III, vi–vii. Compare III, vi, 46–47, and III, vi, 36–41, especially 37–38, with the fragment, especially with fragment vii, 58. Once more, in both III, vi–vii, and the fragment we have an impressive use of the figure of the Wheel. Compare III, vi, 32–33, with the fragment, vi, 1. Yet again, in III, vi–vii, we have the horrible lustful giant twins, Argante and Olyphant, who certainly represent Aristotle's "unnatural vice," as is clear from a comparison of III, vii, 47–50, with the *Nicomachean Ethics*, Book VII, and who are descendants of Titan, who fought against Jove. They "feed [their] fancy with delightful change." In the fragment, Change, or Mutability, is a descendant of Titan, who fought against Jove. Important ideas in both III, vi–vii, and the fragment, vi–vii, are Nature, cyclic Change, Time, and Death.

If one could accept the printer's improbable conjecture that "Mutability" is a moral discussion on Constancy, that would be another reason for placing the fragment in Book II or III, in both of which Spenser discusses Constancy. If the fragment is on Constancy in the moral sense of Continence and Steadfastness, it is on Temperance or Chastity, and belongs to Book II or III. Spenser would certainly not write another Book so like Temperance and Chastity.

How would the fragment fit in the Book on Justice? Nothing impressed the Renaissance like the rise and fall of individual men, the downfall of men at the height of their prosperity, the turn of the wheel of Fortune. Now in canto v of Book V, which the fragment, according to the numbering of its cantos, would follow, Artegall, the hero of the Book and the equal of Arthur, has fallen from the state of one of the greatest knights in the world to that of bond servant to a woman. She has degraded him from his rank of Chivalry, dressed him in women's weeds, and set him to do woman's work. But Artegall is not merely the hero of a tale. He is Arthur, Lord Grey, who had been Spenser's personal friend, patron, and hero in real life. How naturally, then, would the opening stanza of canto vi of the fragment follow Artegall's fall in canto v of Book V, especially in view of the fact that Spenser habitually begins a canto with reflections on the preceding one:

> What man that sees the ever-whirling wheele
> Of Change, the which all mortall things doth sway,
> But that therby doth find, and plainly feele,
> How Mutability in them doth play
> Her cruell sports, to many mens decay?

The proem might not be written until the canto was finished, as is indicated by the fact that the "unperfite" canto viii has no proem. The word "decay" would not necessarily mean death, for the same word is applied in V, v, to those who, like Artegall, have fallen from knighthood and become subject to Radigund.[1] Perhaps the references to Fortune in V, iv, 47; V, v, 5; V, v, 36, and V, v, 38, are too much the usual thing in Spenser to be significant, though Radigund's and Artegall's anxiety as to how Fortune will decide their combat seems so.

But Artegall represents also Justice. His downfall, therefore, represents in some sense the miscarriage of Justice. Does it suggest the recall of Lord Grey from the Lord-Deputyship of Ireland and the reversal of his policy by Sir John Perrot, which, as we know, from the last canto of Book V, and especially from Spenser's *Veue of the Present State of Ireland*, the poet condemned? We are told that Radigund's treatment of Artegall is just, because he had given his word that if she defeated him he would obey her; but we are made to feel that it is contemptible. If following cantos were rejected, V, v, might be changed; but even as it now stands, woman's government, save Elizabeth of course, is plainly condemned as against Nature.[2]

The probability of the rejection of the fragment on the ground of tact or patriotism will now be clear. If the long discussion of Change, or Mutability, grew out of the downfall of Artegall at the hand of a woman and Artegall's humiliation under woman's government, so that the discussion would be likely to suggest not only a condemnation of Lord Grey's recall but also of Elizabeth's government, it might well occur to Spenser, on second thought, or be suggested to him by Raleigh, that here is a delicate matter. And the

---

[1] V, v, 21.   [2] V, v, 25.

same would be true if the discussion of Mutability grew out of any similar event. Again, the Cynthia, or Phoebe, or Diana, of the fragment could not fail to suggest Elizabeth, not only because all the court commonly used these terms to flatter Elizabeth, but also because Spenser himself had so used them in the *Faerie Queene* and had pointed out in the letter to Raleigh that they did refer to Elizabeth. In view of this fact, the nineteen-stanza account, in the fragment, of Faunus' spying on Diana at her bath might, for example, be a reason for the rejection of the fragment.

I have tried to suggest that the fragment called "Mutability" may have been written as a part of one of the completed books of the *Faerie Queene*. If it be argued that it does not fit perfectly in any of them, this answer seems worthy of consideration: Spenser probably rejected it just because it did not fit perfectly.

Finally, the long discussion of Change, or Mutability, might conceivably have grown out of the downfall of some great character in the "other part" of the *Faerie Queene*, which was to deal with political virtues. But in the absence of any books on political virtues, this solution seems improbable.

We come now to the question of Aristotle's influence on "Mutability." Here it will be well to review the plot of the poem. Change has brought sin and death and injustice into the world, and subdued the earth to her rule. Having done this much, she aspires to rule the heavens. She begins by attempting to displace Cynthia, or Phoebe, or Diana, the moon-goddess. Jove interferes, and Mutability boldly tells him that she intends to have his throne too, and all the gods'. She bases her claim on the fact that she is a descendant of Titan, whom Jove had dispossessed. Jove starts to try the case; but Mutability, feeling that he would be partial to his own interest, appeals to the God of Nature. Heaven and Earth assemble, and Nature takes the judgment seat. In addition to her claim through inheritance, Mutability, or Change, pleads that in reality she is the supreme ruler; for earth, air, fire, water; seasons, months, day and night; life and death; the planets in the heavens; and even the gods, including Jove himself, are subject to her law of change. Nature is long silent, but at length gives her decision in few words. It is true, she says, that all things hate steadfastness, and are changed.

But essentially they are not changed. They change in a cycle; "they are not changed from their first estate"; they only dilate their being and perfect themselves. Change does not rule over them; "but they raigne over change, and do their states maintaine." Mutability shall not displace Jove, but shall give up her aspirations and content herself to be ruled by Nature. Thus shall Change be governed until the time comes when we shall all be changed. After that there will be no more Change.

Several of the ideas of the fragment are strikingly like those of Aristotle. For example, the idea of cyclic Change and of the rule of Nature is repeatedly expressed in the *Nicomachean Ethics* and in the *Politics*. In *Politics* VIII, xii, Aristotle says:

> In the *Republic* the subject of revolutions is discussed by Socrates, but not satisfactorily. For there is no particular treatment of the revolution incident to his best or primary polity. He assigns as a cause the fact that nothing in the world is permanent; all things change in a certain cycle, ...

Again, in *Politics*, Book I, Aristotle discusses at length the rule and subordination which is in accordance with Nature. He shows that the principle of rule and subordination prevails throughout Nature. For example, he says:

> Wherever several parts combine to form one common whole . . . . the relation of ruler and subject invariably manifests itself. And this fact which is characteristic of animate things is true of Nature generally; for even in inanimate things there is a sort of rule and subordination, e.g. in harmony.[1]

Connected with Spenser's fragment, and with Aristotle's study of virtue, there is an interesting bit of theology. It is "mortall" things, Spenser tells us in the very first sentence of the fragment and throughout the poem, that are subject to Change. In that happy condition before Change broke the laws of Nature and brought sin and death into the world, that is, before man became mortal, man and all things enjoyed a state which was without change and without motion.[2] And, Spenser tells us, clearly with a part of the fifteenth chapter of First Corinthians in mind,

> Time shall come that all shall changed be,
> And from thenceforth, none no more change shall see.

[1] *Politics*, I, v.

[2] Compare the opening stanzas of the fragment, especially stanzas 5 and 6, with the close, especially vii, 59, and viii, 2.

In other words, there is to be a return to the pre-Mutability state. Then, commenting on this fact, which is announced by Nature, Spenser says:

> Then gin I think on that which Nature sayd,
> Of that same time when *no more Change* shall be,
> But *steadfast rest* of all things *firmly stayd*
> Upon the *pillours* of *Eternity*,
> That is *contrayr to Mutabilitie:*
> For, all that *moveth*, doth in *Change* delight:
> *But* thence-forth all shall *rest* eternally
> With Him that is the God of *Sabbaoth* hight:
> *O that great Sabbaoth God*, graunt me that
> Sabaoths sight.[1]

At the close of Book VII of the *Nicomachean Ethics* Aristotle gives a brief and unmistakably clear expression of this doctrine of a changeless and motionless state of bliss. It precisely matches, in this respect, the closing stanza of Spenser's poem on Mutability, or Change. It is as follows:

The same thing is never constantly pleasant to us, as our nature is not simple, but there exists in us a sort of second nature, which makes us *mortal* beings. Thus if one element is active, it acts against the nature of the other, and when the two elements are in equilibrium, the action appears to be neither painful nor pleasant. If there were a being, whose nature is simple, the same action would always be *supremely pleasant* to him.

It is thus that God enjoys one simple pleasure everlastingly; for there is an *activity* not only of *motion* but of *immobility*, and pleasure consists rather in *rest* than in *motion*.

Much of Aristotle's teaching concerning the active and the speculative life, and the superiority of the latter, had probably become so merged with Christian teaching as to lose its identity. The emphasis placed by Spenser on a motionless state of bliss, at the close of "Mutability," suggests, however, that the poet had particularly in mind the ideas which we have just quoted from Aristotle—not solely the common doctrines of the church on eschatology. And this is the more probable in view of the fact that, as we saw when studying the *Faerie Queene*, Spenser had elsewhere made frequent use, not only of the ideas of the *Nicomachean Ethics*, but of this very book.

---

[1] "Mutability," viii, 2.

There are two modern works which conceivably may have had some influence on the fragment called "Mutability." Professor Oliver Elton, in *Modern Studies*,[1] says, "With all [their] difference of spirit, we seem to find an echo of Bruno in Spenser's ["Mutability"]." He has in mind mainly the *Spaccio de la Bestia trionfante*, which, he finds, was written and published during Bruno's stay in England, 1584–85.

The *Spaccio* is an allegorical proposal for the overthrow of the current social ethics and the establishment of a fresh code of human excellence. There is first a vague catastrophe. Then the reigning vices and follies, which are represented by the constellations, are displaced by virtues. This new heaven represents a new society on earth.

The scene is Olympus. The highly immoral Jove, feeling age and impotency coming on, and dreading death, and change into something which shall have no memory of Jove, decides on a reformation, especially of other people. On the anniversary of the fall of the giants he calls the gods together and requires them to show repentance by completely changing the chart of the heavens. This change is the dispatch of the triumphant beast, which consists of all the old constellations, that is, of all vices and follies. Jove perseveres until the whole heavens have been changed, each vice being displaced by its opposite virtue.

Professor Elton finds that both Spenser and Bruno play with large conceptions of change and recurrence, and both present a conclave of the gods led by Jove and discomfited by the feeling of decay. The machinery of the two pieces is alike thus far. But the idea of cyclic change which essentially is not change is absent from Bruno's allegory. Professor Elton admits that the idea is an old one, but finds that it had been rephrased in Bruno's *Eroici Furori*. Bruno's rephrasing of this idea, which Professor Elton quotes, is as follows:

Death and dissolution do not befit this entire mass, of which the star that is our globe consists. Nature as a whole cannot suffer annihilation; and thus, at due times, in fixed order, she comes to renew herself, changing and altering all her parts; and this it is fitting should come with fixity of succession, every part taking the place of all the other parts. . . . . Thus all things in their kind have the vicissitudes of lordship and slavery, felicity and infelicity, of the state that is called life, and the state that is called death; of light and darkness, and of good and evil. And there is nothing which by natural fitness is eternal but the substance which is matter.[1]

Concerning the first point of similarity to which Professor Elton calls attention, namely, that both writers play with large conceptions of change and recurrence, this may be said: If this fact proves that Bruno influenced Spenser, then Bruno's influence on Spenser was far-reaching. For not only does Spenser discuss change in everything he wrote; but he several times deals with large conceptions of change and recurrence. In the *Faerie Queene*, III, vi, 36 ff., for example, Spenser tells how all things take their substances from Chaos; catch a form; pass into life; live, die, decay, and return to Chaos; only to pass into other forms:

> For in the wide wombe of the world there lyes,
> In hatefull darknesse and in deepe horrore,
> An huge eternal Chaos, which supplyes
> The substances of natures fruitfull progenyes.

> All things from thence doe their first being fetch,
> And borrow matter, whereof they are made,
> Which when as forme and feature it does ketch,
> Becomes a bodie, and doth then invade
> The state of life, out of the griesly shade.
> That substance is eterne, and bideth so,
> Ne when the life decayes, and forme does fade,
> Doth it consume, and into nothing go,
> But changed is, and often altred to and fro.

> The substance is not chaunged, nor altered,
> But th' only forme and outward fashion;
> For every substance is conditioned
> To change her hew, and sundry formes to don,
> Meet for her temper and complexion:
> For formes are variable and decay.

There follows a discussion of the enemy, "wicked Time." See in the same canto, 46–47, the account of the lover, who

> All be he subject to mortalitie,
> Yet is eterne in mutabilitie,
> And by succession made perpetuall.

---

[1] *Modern Studies*, p. 33.

Again, in the long prologue to the Book on Justice, see Spenser's account, not only of the change from the age when all were just to the present age of injustice, but also of vast changes in the heavens, which changes are related to the moral change.   Even the sun,

> Foure times his place he shifted hath in sight,
> And twice hath risen, where he now doth West,
> And wested twice, where he ought rise aright.

Once more, in the second canto of the Book on Justice, 29 ff., we have an argument and reply strikingly like those in the fragment called "Mutability." The Gyant with the "huge great paire of ballance" justifies a political revolution on the ground that earth, fire, air, and water have all encroached on each other.   The decision, given by the Knight of Justice, is that the change is only apparent; in reality they have not encroached on each other.

Another thing may safely be said: It is not necessary to suppose that Spenser got his machinery from Bruno.   Not only was Spenser writing on change long before there was any possibility of influence from Bruno; but the theme was a favorite one in the Middle Ages and especially in the Renaissance.[1]   See, for example, at the end of the "Two other very Commendable Letters," now printed with the *Faerie Queene*, "Certaine Latin Verses, of the frailtie and Mutability of all things, saving only Vertue."   These "Verses" were printed in 1580, four years before Bruno's allegory was written and five years before it was published.   Concerning the fact that both Spenser and Bruno describe "a conclave of the gods led by Jove," an important part of the second of Professor Elton's two points of similarity, it may be answered that Spencer describes such a conclave in his *Muiopotmos*.   Moreover, we have here not only a conclave, but a trial, as is the case in the fragment called "Mutability." There is a debate between Minerva and Neptune as to who shall be god of Athens.   Jove tries the case in the presence of the assembled gods.   It should be added here that a conclave of the gods is a commonplace in literature.   It has been a popular theme since the days of Homer and Virgil.   See *Aeneid* x and *Demeter*, vss. 313 ff.   See

---

[1] See, for example, the *Romance of the Rose*, Ellis' tr., pp. 170–71 and 208–64, or Chaucer's *Troilus and Criseyde* or *Monks Tale*.   See also *Mod. Lang. Notes*, VIII (1893), 230 ff. and 235 ff., and *Pub. Mod. Lang. Assoc.*, VIII (1893), 303 ff., and Neilson's *Court of Love* and Chambers' *Medieval Stage*.

also Triggs's edition of Lydgate's *Assembly of Gods*, 1905, E.E.T.S., Introduction, pp. lii ff., and O. H. Moore's article in *Mod. Phil.*, XVI (1918), 170. It ought to be said further that in Bruno's allegory there is no trial, and Change is not personified. And, finally, so far as cyclic change is concerned, it is found, as we have already seen, in Aristotle.

There is another piece of modern writing which may possibly have influenced the machinery of Spenser's fragment: *The Rare Triumphs of Love and Fortune.* This play is in places strikingly like Spenser's fragment called "Mutability." There is a quarrel between Venus and Fortune as to how much power each has, the quarrel being started by Fortune. The two goddesses appear before Jupiter and the assembled gods to argue the case. After some argument Jupiter decides to allow Fortune and Venus to try their powers on a pair of faithful lovers, Fortune to do her worst and Venus her best, and the one who shows the greatest might to be allowed the sovereignty. First one and then the other seems superior, until finally Jupiter decides that in this and all other cases they must compromise and not thwart each other. They unite to make the lovers happy. An interesting argument made by Fortune is her assertion that all things—the sea, the air, even the heavens, the stars—feel her scars.[1]

It will be observed that this play is like Spenser's fragment in several particulars. In the play, as in Spenser's poem, Fortune is personified; it is Fortune who starts the contest; there is a trial; and the trial is presided over by Jupiter, or Jove, in the presence of the assembled gods. The decision is much like that in the fragment; just as in the fragment Change must operate in accordance with Nature, so in the *Rare Triumph of Love and Fortune* the two contestants must henceforth work in harmony. And, finally, both in the play and in Spenser's fragment, Fortune, or Change, bases her claim to sovereignty on the argument that the sea, the air, even the heavens, the stars, feel her might.

I know of nothing which makes it improbable that Spenser should have read *The Rare Triumphs of Love and Fortune.* There are facts which make it doubtful whether he ever saw Bruno's

[1] For this play see *Dodsley's Old English Plays*, Hazlitt, Vol. VI.

Spaccio and *Furori*. As Professor Elton admits, Bruno's works made little if any impression on England until long after Bruno and Spenser were dead; they were not studied even by small and select circles. From all that is known of Sidney's life and thought and character—and much is known—we may be sure that Sidney could have had no sympathy with the teachings of the *Spaccio*. Spenser was in Ireland during Bruno's stay in England. It is not impossible that Sidney, to whom the *Spaccio* was dedicated, may have sent Bruno's allegory to Spenser, as Professor Elton suggests, though if he had read it before sending it he would have found its teachings repulsive to himself and would have known they would be so to Spenser.

But whether Spenser read Bruno or *The Rare Triumphs of Love and Fortune*, or both, this much is certain: he did not draw his ethical teaching or his theology from them. *The Rare Triumphs of Love and Fortune* is not an ethical or theological discussion. The *Spaccio* is a study of ethical and theological matters; but its teachings are diametrically opposed to Spenser's views. The whole spirit of the *Spaccio* is opposed to Spenser's thought and nature, as Professor Elton recognized. Spenser is chivalric; Bruno is, in the *Spaccio*, realistic, to the extent of the frankest recognition of human needs. Spenser is reverent; Bruno is irreverent, impious. Spenser everywhere makes loving use of the Old and New Testaments, and he thinks of the Deity and of the pagan gods as having human form and attributes; Bruno is violently against Jewish and anthropomorphic theology. Professor Elton fully recognizes that Bruno's teachings could not appeal to Spenser. For example, he says, "His [Bruno's] ethics did not appeal to Spenser," the singer of Chivalry; and again, "The ethical ideal that results [from the study in the *Spaccio*] is . . . . a corrective to that set forth in the *Faerie Queene*."

It appears, then, that although the discussion of "Mutability" in the fragment forms in no proper sense a part of Spenser's treatment of the "twelve moral virtues of Aristotle," it is composed of ideas derived from Aristotle—ideas discussed by him in close connection with the virtues, moral and political.

A VEUE OF THE PRESENT STATE OF IRELAND

Spenser's *A Veue of the Present State of Ireland* is a practical state paper. It has the definite object of justifying Lord Grey and his policy and deploring the reversal of that policy. It is not a proposal for the establishment of an ideal government, but for dealing with conditions which are already fixed—such as the state of civilization of the Irish, the great difference between the Irish and the English peoples, and the government of the former people by the latter. It is not a theoretical discussion of morality and politics.

Nevertheless there are everywhere throughout the *Veue* reflections from Aristotle. Indeed the practical nature of the *Veue* is itself justified by arguments which are to be found in some of Aristotle's more practical chapters. In the *Veue*, Spenser's characters, Eudoxus and Irenius, speak as follows, Irenius representing Spenser's own opinion:

Eudox.: Her Majestie may yet, when it shall please her, alter anything of thos former ordinances, or appoynt other lawes, that may be more both for her own behoofe, and for the good of that people.

Iren.: Not so: for it is not so easy, now that things are growne into an habit and have ther certain course, to change the channell, and turn ther streames an other way; for they may have now a collourable pretence to withstand such innovasion, having accepted other lawes and rules alredy.

Eudox.: As for the lawes of England, they are surely most just and most agreeable both with the government and with the nature of the people: how falls it out then, that you seme to dislike of them, as not so meete for that realm of Ireland, and not onely the common law, lent also the statutes and acts of parlament, which were specially provided and intended for the onely benefit thereof.

Iren.: I was shewing you by what means, and in what sort, the positive lawes were first brought in and established by the Norman Conqueror; which were not by him devised, nor applyed to the state of the realme then being, nor as it might best be, (as should by lawgivers be principally regarded,) but were indede the very lawes of his owne country of Normandy: the condicon whereof, how far it differeth from this of England, is apparent to every least judgment. But to transfer the same lawes for the governing of the realm of Ireland, was much more inconvenient and unmete: In Ireland . . . . they were otherwise effected, and yet not so remayned, so as the same lawes, me seemes, can ill fit with their disposicion, or work that reformacon that is wished: for lawes ought to be fashioned unto the manners and condicons of the people, to whom they are ment, and not to be imposed upon them according to the simple rule of right . . . . ffor he that would transfer the lawes of the Lacedemonians to the people of Athens should find a great absurdity and inconvenience, ...[1]

. . . .

Iren.: I doe not thinke yt convenient, though . . . . to change all the lawes and make newe; for that should bread great trouble and confusione, aswell in the Englishe now dwellinge and to be planted, as alsoe in the Irishe. For the Englishe, having bene trained upp alwayes in the English government, will hardly be enduced unto any other, and the Irishe wilbe better drawne to the Englishe, then the Englishe to the Irishe governmente. Therefore since wee cannot nowe applie lawes fitt to the people, as in the first institutione of commone-welthes it ought to be, wee will applye the people, and fitt them to the lawes, as it most conveniently maye be. The lawes therefore we resolve shall abyde in the sam sorte that they doe, both Commone Lawes and Statutes, onely suche defects in the Comone Lawe, and inconveniens in the Statutes, as in the beginninge wee noted, and as men of deep insights shall advise, may be changed by other newe actes and ordynances to be by a Parlyamente there confirmed.[2]

Compare this with the following passages from Aristotle's *Politics:*

Alterations [of the laws] seem to require no little caution. Where the improvement is but slight compared with the evil of accustoming the citizens lightly to repeal the lawes, it is undoubtedly our duty to pass over some mistakes whether of the legislature or the executive, as the benefit we shall derive from the alteration will not be equal to the harm we shall get by accustoming ourselves to disobey authority. . . . . For all the potency of the law to secure obedience depends upon habit, and habit can only be formed by lapse of time; so that the ready transition from the existing laws to others that are new is a weakening of the efficacy of law itself.[3]

. . . .

The good legislator and the true statesman should keep his eyes open not only to the absolutely best polity but also to the polity which is best under the actual conditions. . . . . He should understand the polity which is

---

[1] Grosart's edition, lines 390–444.
[2] *Ibid.*, lines 6176–98.
[3] *Politics*, II, viii.

most appropriate to the mass of states, especially as the great majority of political writers, even if successful in their treatment of the other points, utterly miss the mark of practical utility. For it is not only the absolutely best polity which is the proper subject of consideration, but also that which is possible in any given case. . . . . But our modern writers either aspire to the highest polity, for which a number of external advantages are indispensable, or, if they describe a form more generally attainable, put out of sight all existing forms except the favored one and pronounce a panegyric upon the Lacedaemonian or some other polity. What we want however is to introduce some new system which the world will easily be induced and enabled to accept as an innovation upon the existing forms. . . . .

The true statesman should be capable of coming to the rescue of existing polities. . . . . He should discern the best laws and the laws appropriate to each form of polity, as it is the laws enacted which should be, and in fact are universally relative to the polities rather than the polities to the laws.[1]

The passages quoted from Spenser will show the practical nature and something of the scope of the *Veue*. A comparison of the excerpts from the *Veue* with those from the *Politics* will show that Aristotle's and Spenser's ideas are practically identical. It will be noted that both writers are opposed to changing the laws save for weighty reasons; that both stress the importance of habit in connection with obedience to the law; that both make a distinction between the ideally perfect polity and the best government that may be had under given conditions, and hold that the lawmaker should give consideration to the latter; that both recognize that it is necessary to consider what kind of government or laws a people can be induced to accept; and that both insist that the laws ought to be adapted to the particular polity or government for which they are intended. Besides the agreement in principle, there are certain agreements in detail which indicate that Spenser had the *Politics* in mind. In the discussion from which the excerpts are taken, Spenser, like Aristotle, names Solon, Lycurgus, and the Lacedaemonians. Again Spenser refers to the warlike nature of the Lacedaemonians, as Aristotle does in an earlier passage. Yet again, in insisting that the laws should be adapted to the polity for which they are meant, Aristotle complains that

our modern writers either aspire to the highest polity, for which a number of external advantages are indispensable, or, if they describe a form more

[1] *Politics*, VI, 1.

generally attainable, put out of sight all existing forms except the favored one and pronounce a panegyric upon the Lacedaemonian or some other polity;

and Spenser, in making the same point, says,

Lawes ought to be fashioned unto the manners and condicons of the people, to whom they are ment, and not to be imposed upon them according to the simple rule of right . . . . ffor he that would transfer the lawes of the Lacedaemonians to the people of Athens should find a great absurdity and inconvenience.

Such points of resemblance to Aristotle as we have here pointed out are to be found throughout the *Veue,* in connection with the discussion of education,[1] the supremacy of the law,[2] and many other topics.

---

[1] Compare the *Veue,* ed. A. B. Grosart, pp. 27, 28, 238, 239, with the *Politics,* V, i; IV, xiv, xv; II, v; and VIII, ix.

[2] Compare the *Veue,* p. 59, with the *Politics,* III, xv, xvi; II, ix; and III, xi.

THE SHEPHEARDES CALENDER AND THE MINOR POEMS

Much of the serious matter in *The Shepheardes Calender* and the minor poems is ecclesiastical. Nevertheless, the influence of Aristotle is unmistakable.

In the *Calender* the July eclogue is plainly Aristotelian. It teaches the doctrine of the mean. For this opinion we do not have to depend upon Thomalin's emblem: "In medio virtus"; or upon E. K.'s statement, in the gloss, that, "He taketh occasion to prayse the meane and lowly state . . . . according to the saying of olde Philosophers, that vertue dwelleth in the middest, being environed with two contrary vices." The teaching of the eclogue itself is too clear to be misunderstood. But not only does the eclogue teach the Aristotelian doctrine of the mean; it teaches the mean concerning ambition, which mean is one of the Aristotelian virtues.

Again, in the October eclogue there is Aristotelian influence. Spenser refers to the influence of music on the soul, and E. K. cites Aristotle and Plato as authorities on the subject. For Aristotle's long discussion of the influence of music on the soul and character see the *Politics*, V, v.

Spenser's *Fowre Hymnes* are Platonic, as all ambitious love poetry of the period was expected to be; but throughout the rest of the minor poems there is a more or less important Aristotelian influence. For example, in *Mother Hubberds Tale*, lines 143 to 145, Aristotle's two standards of right, political and natural justice, are named:

> There is no right in this partition,
> Ne was it so by institution,
> Ordained first, ne by the law of Nature.

Again, in *Muiopotmos*, line 178, "All change is sweet," reflects Aristotle's "But change, as the poet says, is 'the sweetest thing in the world.'"[1] Yet again, in *Mother Hubberds Tale*, lines 126 and 1131, we have as a standard the Aristotelian "rule of reason."

[1] *Nicomachean Ethics*, VII, xv.

This brings to a close my study of the influence of Aristotle's *Politics* and *Ethics* on Spenser. To the argument that any given point of similarity between Aristotle and Spenser may be purely a coincidence there is no answer. But these points of similarity are too numerous to be the result of chance. Aristotle certainly had a very considerable influence on Spenser.